LIKE TO THE LARK

The Chess Picture by Karel van Mander, 1604

LIKE TO THE LARK

THE EARLY YEARS OF SHAKESPEARE

BY FREDERICK J. POHL

Clarkson N. Potter, Inc./Publisher NEW YORK

DISTRIBUTED BY CROWN PUBLISHERS, INC.

PRINTED IN GREAT BRITAIN

CONTENTS

ACKNOWLEDGMENTS

I PARTICULARLY WISH TO THANK GERALDINE HUSTON (Mrs. Horace Huston) of Teaneck, New Jersey, for suggesting the title of this book and for several ideas dealt with in it. Professor Celeste T. Wright, Ph.D., Department of English at Davis, University of California, a poet, a specialist in Elizabethan studies, and a one-time editor, gave unsparingly of her time in making detailed suggestions. I am indebted to Professor Elliot L. Gilbert, Ph.D., Department of English at Davis, University of California, and to his wife Sandra Gilbert, Ph.D., and to Professor Markel Weidhorn, Ph.D., Department of English at Yeshiva University, for their scholarly and practical advice.

I have acknowledged in the text of this book the stimulus received from Professor Irving Linn, Ph.D., of Yeshiva University, specialist in the evolution of the English language. I have also

vii

acknowledged the advice given me by Dr. James B. McManaway, Director of the Folger Shakespeare Memorial Library and Editor of *Shakespeare Quarterly*.

I am indebted to Dr. Harold Hough, Dean Emeritus of Drew Theological Seminary, for calling my attention to the influence John Shakespeare's sacrifice of career must have had on the character of his son William; and I owe much to Professor Stanley Rypins, Ph.D., Professor of English Emeritus at Brooklyn College, for his wise counsel. Deeply appreciated encouragement came from Professor Ernest F. Amy, Ph.D., Professor of English Emeritus at Ohio Wesleyan University; Professor Jay Halio, Ph.D., Department of English, University of Delaware; Mr. John Hammond, one-time Managing Editor of New York University Press; Mr. Robert T. King, Director of South Carolina University Press; and Miss Dorothy Gilbert, poet and college teacher of English. I thank my friend Mr. Arthur Godfrey of Pictou, Nova Scotia, a life-long student of Shakespeare, for invaluable conversations and correspondence through many years.

I pay tribute to the staff who served my needs in the New York Public Library and in the Reading Room of the British Museum. The meticulous and constructive labors of my editors, Mrs. Irene Noonan and Mrs. Jane West must not go unsung. Above all, I am grateful to my wife Josephine for her unfailing support that steeled me to persevere in the face of opposition from inflexible conservatives.

LIKE TO THE LARK

1

PUZZLES

" Attend, and mark:
I do hear the morning lark."

MIDSUMMER NIGHT'S DREAM, 4.1.99

T HE EIGHTEENTH CENTURY ESTABLISHED THE BARD idolatry in Stratford. To those who wished to know what Shakespeare looked like, Stratford folk pointed with pride to the bust in the chancel of their church. But that bust in Stratford Church was mistreated by destructive hands during Cromwellian disorders, presumably in 1649. We know with practical certainty what happened to it.[1] The head was knocked off by the Puritans, and when it struck the pavement the tip of the nose was broken, and one of the cheeks was dented. In the third decade of the eighteenth century the face of the bust was resculptured to remove evidence of the damage: the nose was shortened a quarter of an inch; the cheeks were reduced to conceal the injury to one of them; the reduction of the cheeks permitted replacing the original and outmoded down-turned mustache with an upturned mustache in the fashion of the

1

repairer's day; and fourth and final effrontery, when the wide-spread eyeballs were found to extend out too far in relation to the reduced cheeks, the outer half of each eyeball was chiselled down, making the eyeballs smaller and their centers closer together.

Though thus wretchedly metamorphosed, the bust in Stratford Church continued to be looked upon as a likeness of Shakespeare. Therefrom came mischief.

David Garrick asked his friend, the portrait painter Thomas Gainsborough, to produce a composite picture of Garrick and Shakespeare with as close a likeness to each as possible. Gainsborough in 1768 journeyed to Stratford to see the bust. He wrote perceptively to Garrick: "Shakespeare's bust is a silly smiling thing." He also looked perceptively at the Droeshout engraving in the First Folio, and wrote of it: "A stupider face I never beheld. . . . It is impossible that such a mind and ray of heaven could shine with such a face and a pair of eyes as that picture has."[2]

Gainsborough was, of record, the first discriminating person to observe that both the preposterous Droeshout engraving and the bizarre bust in Stratford Church were inane and spiritless.

Since these reputed likenesses did not appear to be portraits of the same man but of two different men, an inevitable question arose. Was there something phony about the identity of the poet? Had a hoax been palmed off on the world? If the author of the plays in the First Folio looked like the Droeshout engraving, then Shakespeare of Stratford, if he looked like the bust in Stratford Church, could not have been the playwright. In that case, who was? Were two different men involved—William Shakespeare of Stratford, believed to be the poet-dramatist, and some other unknown man who was the real author? The new heresy was soon voiced. The next year, 1769, saw the first published skepticism as to Shakespeare's authorship presented in the anonymous *The Life and Adventures of Common Sense: An Historical Allegory*, believed to have been written by Herbert Lawrence, a friend of Garrick's. The hero of the book writes plays which are passed off by an intellectual thief, the Stratford actor, William Shakespeare, as his own. Thus, born out of the dissimilarity of two portraits, the Great Suspicion was launched. It so grew in people's minds that many theories of substitute authorship have been broached, all of them attempts to solve what some people have sincerely felt to be a puzzle.

The idea that the Stratford actor was not the poet-dramatist was warmly welcomed by the cultural descendants of those university wits who had been the poet's first detractors. William Shakespeare had never been forgiven for being England's supreme genius and yet a seller of a "commoditie," a man who had actually worked with his hands. He had left grammar school in his early teens, never went to college or improved himself by listening to university lecturers. In short, he was a vulgar newcomer who had no noble blood in his veins. From the point of view of many English aristocrats he was an impossibility, and, indeed, intellectual snobbery has propounded most of the sixty-four theories of substitute authorship. All the theories have elements of sensationalism in that they challenge a cherished conception, are bold and provocative and delude the uninformed with plausible claims of factual support. Because they have seemed to fill a need, they have captivated millions of readers.

The substitute candidates include five earls (Derby, Devonshire, Oxford, Rutland, Southampton), two countesses (Oxford, Pembroke), a combination of three of the above, a combination of the entire seven, and "The Great Unknown." There are some candidates among commoners: a woman of Warwickshire (Anne Whatley); a gentleman scholar (Antony Bacon, elder brother of Sir Francis); an Italian of whom nothing whatsoever is known (Mercutio Florio); fifteen contemporary poets (Lyly, Peele, Greene, Kyd, Marlowe, Lodge, Nash, Daniel, Chapman, Chettle, Munday, Jonson, Heywood, Webster, Middleton), each as author of part or all of Shakespeare's plays; an unknown "kept poet"; and a group of Jesuits, according to a Catholic theory. The mentality that demanded noble blood for genius made it logical that someone write a book claiming Queen Elizabeth had dashed off the poems and plays in the midst of her political duties and social engagements. After that it was no surprise to be told that Shakespeare's works were written by a Jew, a theory which Jewish friends say "had to happen sooner or later." An even later theory, quite in character with its originators, is that Shakespeare's works were written—you should guess it—by a Russian. Can absurdity go further? No doubt it will.

William F. Friedman, the professional cryptologist who broke the Japanese code, demolished the pretensions of the "buried" Francis Bacon ciphers, in *The Shakespearean Ciphers Examined*, 1957. His book

3

has been hailed by orthodox scholars as a very welcome weapon. Sir Francis Bacon, however, is no longer the favorite candidate for substitute authorship. Newer theories have produced candidates more flavorsome than Bacon. They impress people who love the esoteric. One can scarcely discuss the Bard in public without being asked: "Who wrote Shakespeare?"

While the inadequacies and incongruences of the portraits were the historical first cause for the feeling that the Stratford man could not have been the poet-dramatist, that feeling has been intensified by orthodox biographers who have overstressed what they call the "Lost Years" of Shakespeare's adolescence and early manhood. In their demand for "scientific proof" and in their refusal to entertain reasonable suppositions regarding Shakespeare's formative years, they have made his development from Stratford boy to successful playwright in the London theater appear to be an incredible miracle.

Biographers of Shakespeare bemoan the sparsity of biographical facts, even though more is definitely known about Shakespeare than about most Elizabethan poets and playwrights. On the other hand, there has been a desire to solve the obvious mysteries, a desire intensified by the depths and heights of the poet's genius. How did he begin to write? When? Where? From having been a clerk in his father's shop in Stratford until, it was generally believed, about the age of seventeen, how had he become a facile versifier and competent playwright by the time he went to London, which, most scholars agreed, was at about the age of twenty-four? Here were seven formative years about which nothing was known, and many said nothing could be known. One professor called it "probably the most fascinating and baffling enigma in all English literary history."[3]

How did the young man develop writing skills? Was it during his pre-London years? Some thought he began that development only after he came to London. But to suggest that "one of the great creative geniuses of the world wrote nothing—or nothing, apparently, that has survived—until he was twenty-five"[4] merely posed another mystery.

Would it be possible to discover whether Shakespeare wrote poems and plays before he went to London? And if so, what poems and plays?

4   It seemed fatuous to believe that after four centuries it might be

possible to find any answers to these questions. Yet the feeling persisted that the answers might appear if one could determine the order of composition of Shakespeare's earliest works.

While there had been considerable successful research into the sequential order in which most of his plays had first been staged, and while much energy had been expended toward ascertaining when each of his works had first been published, there was ignorance as to the order of composition of his early works. Without knowledge of the order of composition, there could be no valid study of his early development as verse writer or as dramatist. When a professor venturing to trace Shakespeare's stylistic development based his study upon an assumed order of composition and then admitted that "conceivably the order may be reversed," it was obvious that his critical findings were unreliable if not valueless. [5]

Questions that came insistently were these: Could the order of composition of the early works of Shakespeare be ascertained? Could one find a clue to that order in the works themselves? Is it not true in literature as in painting that one may find such a clue in an increasing propensity to some stylistic tendency where the works are unquestionably authentic? Was there some stylistic tendency of which Shakespeare was unaware—some unconscious proclivity which would reveal the order of composition?

I believed there must have been some such proclivity, and that it could be discovered. I began sleuthing, hopefully, but without foreseeing that I would be rewarded by finding three unconscious proclivities in Shakespeare's verse that would establish triply corroborated findings.

When, in a lecture, I first broached the idea of applying statistical measurement to the poetry of Shakespeare, an elderly gentleman in the audience cast off his customary sweetness and wrathfully blasted against what he said would destroy poetic beauty. He feared it would be like a botanist pulling petals off flowers. But when I reminded him that in Shakespeare's day verses had been called "numbers," his feeling of esthetic outrage faded, and he agreed that counting the numbers would in no way be destructive.

We recognize, of course, that "a creative writer does not develop in a mechanical or regular way." [6] This is certainly true in regard to his creativity. The flowering of genius is unpredictable. A

5

lyric poet breaks out into song erratically. He may create three superb lyrics in a row and subsequently write a decidedly inferior one. Creativity has no mechanical or regular progression.

A writer's objective practice in metrics, however, is something different from what we mean by creativity. A practicing artist constantly acquires more skill in technique. Skill in a seriously practiced art is cumulative, and develops with measurable consistency. As will be shown, Shakespeare's stylistic growth had a regular and measurable progression.

For this opinion there were excellent authorities. Sir Edmund Chambers said of metrical tests "which put in statistical form the relative frequencies in each play of certain features of Shakespeare's versification . . . I do not undervalue these features as elements in determining the chronology of the plays."[7] John Mackinnon Robertson had the prescience to say that in such tests he "detected the open secret of Shakespeare's authentic style."[8] Albert Feuillerat, in comment on Robertson, divined that the method of using "versification as a means of investigation" is both "just" and "penetrating."[9]

Alfred Harbage says the early plays "are the most difficult to date and arrange in chronological order, especially since we have no record of Shakespeare's activities before 1590. . . . It used to be thought that Shakespeare began his career as a dramatist by rewriting the plays of earlier writers. All the supposed evidence for this theory has gradually eroded away, and we are left with the possibility that all the early work is wholly his own."[10]

The words "wholly his own" are a challenge to those who think that in extensive passages of significant length our text is not what Shakespeare himself wrote. If this were the case, statistical measurements would be fruitless. But no one has proved, and I think no one can prove, that the First Folio text is corrupt in poetic passages of sufficient length to upset the comparative percentages upon which my findings are based. The First Folio was edited by Shakespeare's colleagues who used stage versions in their possession, or manuscripts obtained from the playwright's widow. There is every reason to believe that we have the text of each play essentially as Shakespeare wrote it including changes he made at the first staging. Anyone acquainted with theater business knows that when the text of a play that has pleased audiences is revised for revival, the changes made in it are few and slight. "A practicing playwright and actor would not be likely to revise extensively a play after it had been produced."[11] When *Love's Labour's Lost* was advertised as "augmented" and "revised," it was to attract attention to its revival. The revisions, undoubtedly made by Shakespeare because he was present, were in all probability in prose passages, to bring stale jokes up to date. My statistical studies, however, are based exclusively upon the poetry.

As to when most of the early works were written, we have had only guesses. For example, guesses as to the date of composition of *The Comedy of Errors* have ranged over seven years. George Lyman Kittredge guesses and asks us to make our own guess as to any of four years—"1591 to 1594."[12] Peter Alexander dates the comedy "before 1589," though Robert Adger Law scolds him for it.[13] Thomas Whitfield Baldwin persuasively dates it 1588.[14]

Similarly there have been wide-ranging guesses as to the dates of composition of *The Taming of the Shrew*, the three parts of *Henry VI*, *Richard III*, *Love's Labour's Lost*, and *The Two Gentlemen of Verona*. As to the years in which Shakespeare wrote his sonnets, guesses have ranged far more widely—over seventeen years—from 1586 to 1603.

Only one of the first fourteen works of Shakespeare was definitely dated, with a date that everyone accepted. *The Rape of Lucrece* was unquestionably written in 1593–94. *Henry VI, Part 1* appeared to be reliably dated by Nash's "Talbot" reference in 1592 (see Chapter 9). After the stylistic measurements had been made, it was pleasing to find that these two datings served as anchors to the dating of others.

2

FINDINGS

"Why, here begins his morning story right."

THE COMEDY OF ERRORS, 5.1.35

THE STATISTICAL FINDINGS, WHICH ARE THE culmination of several years' research, are tabulated below. The steps by which one arrives at these are fully described in Appendix A, "Sleuthing in Shakespeare" and Appendix B, "Dating the Sonnets." Anyone may easily check their accuracy.

A word of explanation about each of the three stylistic measurements follows: "Percent of open lines" is the percentage of lines which do not need any end punctuation, in the opinion, not of the author, but of the best editors. "Syllabic intensity" is the number of words of three or more syllables per thousand lines of verse. "Pauses per 1,000 lines" are the interruptions to smoothness of flow in Shakespeare's verse. It is a count of all punctuation, except final periods, in speeches or stanzas of six lines or more.

It will be observed that through the years the percent of open lines and the syllabic intensity increase and the pauses decrease.

The three statistical columns that follow corroborate each other in establishing the order of composition of Shakespeare's early works.

	Inferred or anchor date	*Percent of open lines*	*Syllabic Intensity*	*Pause per 1,000 lines*
PASSIONATE PILGRIM, poems 1 to 14	about 1584	6·41	146	1481
VENUS AND ADONIS	as early as 1586	11·76	209	1382
HENRY VI, PART 3	pre-London, about 1587	13.33	206	1391
SONNETS, to Dark Lady, 127 to 152	about 1588	14·50	176	1356
THE COMEDY OF ERRORS	about 1587–88	14·23	209	1346
HENRY VI, PART 2	after arriving in London	15·35	255	1334
THE TAMING OF THE SHREW (same year as *Titus*) 1589		16·16	248	1288
TITUS ANDRONICUS	anchor dated 1589	16·36	248	1281
LOVE'S LABOUR'S LOST	about 1590 or 1591	17·37	(?)	1291
RICHARD III	about 1590 or 1591	17·40	279	1256
SONNETS, 18 to 126	four years centering in 1591	18·30	275	1199
TWO GENTLEMEN OF VERONA	1591 or 1592	18·41	310	1169
HENRY VI, PART 1	(dated by Nash's "Talbot" ref.) 1592	18·35	322	1132
THE RAPE OF LUCRECE	anchor dated 1593–94	19·37	301	1150
ROMEO AND JULIET	1594–95	18·39		
RICHARD II	1595–96	22·66		
MIDSUMMER NIGHT'S DREAM	1595–96	22·62		
SONNETS, first seventeen and last two	about 1596	23·48		1100
KING JOHN	1596–97	27·55		
MERCHANT OF VENICE	1596–97	28·05		
HENRY IV, PART 1	1597	30·48		

After *The Rape of Lucrece*, syllabic intensity ceases to have validity as evidence of sequential order of composition, for by 1595 Shakespeare's syllabic intensity attained a plateau which continued with minor ups and downs to the end of his life. Also, oratorical pauses have not been counted in the later, reliably dated, plays.

The findings are very revealing.

The sudden large jump in Shakespeare's vocabulary, the increase in his use of words of three or more syllables from 209 to 255 in one year, 1588–89, seems to have been the immediate result of his exposure to contacts with playwrights and actors in London.

The early dating of *Venus and Adonis*, instead of the hitherto generally assumed date 1592–93, clears away the confusion that has confronted those who have sought to trace Shakespeare's stylistic development.

The new knowledge of the order of composition of the first four chronicle histories makes possible an insight into how Shakespeare developed as a writer of plays of that type. Similarly, the new knowledge of the order of composition of the first four comedies must be basic to any study of growth in Shakespeare's handling of humor.

The dating of the sonnets to the Dark Lady, and the year in which the poet began writing sonnets to his friend are of superlative biographical importance.

The low syllabic intensity in the sonnets to the Dark Lady calls for an explanation, and such is given in Appendix B.

The closeness of all three findings in *The Taming of the Shrew* and in *Titus Andronicus* establishes that these two plays were unquestionably written within a few months of each other. In consequence, we shall try to find the answer to the much-controverted question as to when and why *The Taming of the Shrew* acquired its present title.

Of all the findings, the most important fact established by the sequential order of composition of Shakespeare's early writings is that he was a facile lyricist before he chose to try his hand at poetic drama. This knowledge opens the way to new insights into the development of what he called his "art," and enables us to perceive for the first time what he meant when he applied that term to his playwriting.

In establishing a hitherto unguessed-at order of composition of the early writings, the findings invalidate those studies of   11

Shakespeare's early development which have been based upon an erroneous order.

In demonstrating that of all the writings that have been published, *The Passionate Pilgrim* and *Venus and Adonis* were Shakespeare's earliest, the statistical findings bring to focus the theme that he made central in those poems and inevitably compel us to consider the bearing that theme had upon his personal experiences in love—experiences passionately recorded in the sonnets.

Knowledge of what Shakespeare wrote before he went to London necessitates a biographical reappraisal of his early career. The findings are a guiding torch into the obscurity of his pre-London years, and justify our taking a new look at the evidences which seem to point to what he did and where he went during those years.

3

STRATFORD

"At seventeen years many their fortunes seek."

AS YOU LIKE IT, 2.3.73

APPENDIX A AND APPENDIX B HAVE TIMED THE singing of the lark. Now we shall watch the lark's ascending flight and listen to the rising song.

We begin by observing young Shakespeare's experiences prior to his writing of *The Passionate Pilgrim* poems.

The poet's father, the son of a farmer (for "it seems almost certain that John Shakespeare was son of Richard Shakespeare in Snitterfield"[1]), married Mary Arden, a gentlewoman descended from a younger son of a leading family in Warwickshire. John took up residence in Stratford, and engaged in the craft of dressing sheep and kid skins, from which he made gloves, girdles, parchment, and purses. An eminently respected tradesman, he rose through various public services to the highest municipal office. By character and ability he became top man in Stratford, what we today call the

13

Mayor. He was addressed as "Mr." (Master) and was eligible to apply for a coat of arms if he wished.

William, the eldest son of John and Mary, was baptized on April 26, 1564. The assumption that William was born on April 23 makes for neatness, since we then have the poet's death in 1616 occurring on his birthday.

For two and one-half years Will Shakespeare was an only child.* When he was four years old, his father as High Bailiff authorized players to give their shows at the Stratford Guild Hall. Strolling players, like mountebanks and charlatans who flocked to country fairs, had been classed with beggars and highwaymen. The law required every man to be a productive worker. Since players were not considered to be productive, they were looked upon as outlaws. In consequence, it had become the custom among the aristocracy who wished to patronize the performing of plays, to license companies of players. A nobleman would lend a group of actors legitimacy by giving them a legal standing as his servants, and they would wear his livery. They were only in small part supported by him, however, and they had to earn most of their living on the road. Thanks to the future dramatist's father, Stratford became a one-day stand for acting companies.

It is natural to believe, though there is no positive evidence for it, that Will Shakespeare attended Stratford Grammar School. Whether he attended that school or some other makes little difference. Sixteenth-century schools were all much alike: harsh and austere, with internal gods of bigotry, pedantry, discipline, and cruelty. The subjects rigorously taught, in addition to Latin as a spoken language, were grammar, dialectic (logic), rhetoric, arithmetic, music, geometry, and astronomy contaminated with astrology. There was very little scientific thinking. Fact and fancy mingled indiscriminately. Emphasis was heavy on the literary and humanistic. History was interlarded with mythology. The kind of education the

* It is to be presumed that Will Shakespeare's parents lavished affection upon him, the more because two previously-born daughters had died in infancy. Before Will was old enough to have been consciously prepared to share his parents' love, his brother Gilbert was born in October of 1566. Some commentators cite *The Passionate Pilgrim*, the *Sonnets*, and *Hamlet*, etc., as evidence that Shakespeare evinced sexual insecurity. The suggestion has been made that such insecurity could be ascribed to a feeling that his mother betrayed him by bringing a rival into his infantile world.[2]

14

future poet obtained depended upon his receptivity and his good judgment in repudiating tomfoolery and useless clutter.

As for the games that boys engaged in during play hours, they were far rougher than our "Safety First" age will allow. Among them were Running the Gauntlet, Balancing a Barrel, dancing, wrestling, stave fighting, jousting, boxing, tumbling.

The death mask which has been established beyond reasonable doubt as that of William Shakespeare of Stratford[3] shows that some time during his life his forehead and scalp had been cut open. The injury is described by J. S. Hart: "$2\frac{1}{4}$ inches back from the eyebrows is a line $2\frac{1}{2}$ inches or $3\frac{1}{2}$ inches long, and running in a diagonal direction across the skull. This shows clearly the existence of a wound, a flesh cut, which has been sewed up, and has healed. The marks of the suture are plainly visible."[4]

The poet's father, as High Bailiff, Justice of the Peace, Queen's Officer, and Judge of the Court of Record, appeared to have an assured future. His career, however, was to be deeply affected by the prejudices of the rival divisions of the Christian religion which pressed menacingly upon many individuals in the kingdom. During the second year of Queen Elizabeth's reign, there had been promulgated as law the so-called Supremacy Oath which required all public officers to swear to recognize in the monarch the "onely supreme governor of this realm, as well in all spiritual or ecclesiastical things or causes, as temporal."[5] By this Tudor invention, Queen Elizabeth, who had no special theological or ecclesiastical training, was placed above all the clergy and bishops. The Queen's avoidance, however, of direct verbal claims to being the Supreme Head of the Church, though in essence that is what the Supremacy Oath made her, was a shrewd, middle-of-the-road compromise. Thus was set the pattern of the Established Church of England. It permitted great latitude in belief, but insisted upon outward conformity. Queen Elizabeth's primary concern was political unity. She personally disapproved of religious reformers more than she did of Papists. Her Secretary, Sir Francis Walsingham, said that what the Queen "seemeth most to dislike of . . . is the progress of religion."[6]

The change from a Catholic to a Protestant mentality in England could not be accomplished by royal decree in a single generation. It took half a century, and in the transition period there was a temporary reversion under the Catholic Queen Mary. Under

15

2*

Queen Elizabeth, the Established Church was active in supporting her Government against conspiracies. In 1570, more than a decade after the Supremacy Oath, a Papal Bull excommunicated and "deposed" Queen Elizabeth. In theory this made English Catholics political traitors, though most of them were sincere patriots, loyal to the Queen as temporal ruler. Anyone who was asked to take the Supremacy Oath and refused was called a recusant. It was the increase of recusancy among the gentry, and particularly among Justices of the Peace, that alarmed the Queen's councillors.

Studies by H. S. Bowden, Sir Edmund Chambers, Herbert Thurston, and John Henry de Groot have established beyond reasonable doubt that John Shakespeare was not only a recusant, but secretly a Papist. Arguments to the contrary are mere suppositions, and all such arguments have been shown to be untenable.*

John Shakespeare was a man of strong ambition. He applied in 1576 for a coat of arms and the status of "Esquier" or "Gentleman." This healthy desire to rise in the world makes all the more significant his sudden sacrifice of everything only a few months later. From January 23, 1577 (New Style), he remained away from meetings of the Stratford Corporation, withdrew completely from the activities of public office, and thus abandoned any hope of political preferment, and with it his application for a coat of arms. His absence from Established Church services made him technically a recusant.

It seems practically certain that the reason John Shakespeare retreated was not financial, but was to avoid being compelled to swear to the Oath of Supremacy which was about to be required of all Queen's Officers and which he could not in conscience take. That Supremacy Oath had not been universally enforced, but in April 1576 a Grand Commission Ecclesiastical was appointed to inquire into infractions of the Supremacy Act. As Chief Alderman, John Shakespeare was in a position to know what was in the wind. The Oath would soon be compulsory for Stratford officials. Indeed, just a few weeks after John Shakespeare began to absent himself from Corporation meetings and to intimate publicly that it was because of financial straits, John Whitgift, a fanatic hater of

* Facts that point to John Shakespeare's having been a recusant are presented by Peter Alexander in *Shakespeare's Life and Art*, p. 21. Facts that leave no other conclusion possible than that John Shakespeare was a Papist are presented by J. H. de Groot in *The Shakespeares and "The Old Faith."*

16

Puritans and Catholics, was appointed Bishop of Worcester. Bent on the persecution of all nonconformists, Whitgift toured his diocese, which included Warwickshire. In Stratford as elsewhere he received no cooperation; for in his report, "he complained that he got no information about recusants worth capture. . . . Recusancy was condoned so generally by the people that no one would inform against them."[7] John Shakespeare was shielded by his fellow townsmen.

The concern which some Protestants have felt over the possibility that William Shakespeare's father had Catholic sympathies has been as petty as any religious prejudice.* It should be enough to please any Protestant that the same scholar (de Groot) who makes the strongest presentation of evidence that John Shakespeare was a Papist is the scholar who most convincingly shows that his poet son was not one.

We now know, with greater certainty than some Stratford townsfolk may have guessed, what were John Shakespeare's innermost thoughts and agonies of soul-searching. He put them in writing in a document which he hid so skillfully that it lay concealed for 180 years. In 1757 a workman who was placing new tiles in the attic of the Shakespeare house in Henley Street found between the rafters and the old tiles a document of six leaves stitched together with pack thread. This was examined in 1790 by the eminent Shakespearean scholar Edmund Malone, who said it was in the handwriting of John Shakespeare. Subsequent skeptics charged that the text was an eighteenth-century fabrication. But in 1923 Herbert Thurston found a Spanish version of its text printed in 1661. After Thurston's discovery, earlier French and Italian versions were found. It is now established that the original text was composed before 1578 by Charles Borromeo, Cardinal of Milan, who prepared it as a formula of devotion to be written by those who would suffer extreme penalties if they openly avowed their Catholic faith. The text was distributed in England by the Jesuit missionaries Edmund Campion and Robert Parsons in 1579 or earlier. John Shakespeare's document, which we know was his because of the dating, was a declaration of faith which must be unseen. It was a private commitment of his cause to the sight of God, a statement of his determination

* If Will Shakespeare attended Stratford Grammar School, the Masters of which were alternatingly Catholics and Protestants, he was exposed to an alternation of points of view which tended to liberalize his mind.[8]

17

to remain true to the old Church, although it might mean torture and death.

John Shakespeare's sacrifice of career for a principle severely handicapped his children. At thirteen years of age William Shakespeare in his private thoughts was probably very critical of his father's stand, since it undermined the family's security and closed doors against the boy's chances for a successful career in Stratford. It no doubt intensified Will's determination to struggle all the harder to achieve fame and fortune.

The emotional impact of his father's sacrifice of all worldly considerations for a privately held belief set before young William Shakespeare, however, an example of personal integrity from which he could never escape, no matter how strongly the allurements of unethical behavior or the lusts of the flesh might tempt him. It is difficult in terms of present-day permissiveness to realize the intensity of the spiritual influence of such a father. John Shakespeare's uncompromising stand conditioned his son to a deeply rooted respect for whatever ideals the future poet himself might cherish. This is the important thing—not what religion the poet's father had but the effect which his devotion to principle had upon the character of his son William.

Also, it must be said, an appreciation of the effect the father's character had upon the son is essential to an understanding of the poet's spiritual struggle depicted in the sonnets.

In regard to the town of Stratford we observe something which is both negative and illuminating. While there are records in or near Stratford of the poet's forebears, of his baptism, betrothal, the birth of his children, his buying of lands and house, and his burial, there is no shred of a record there as to how he developed during the seven years previous to his arrival in London. There is not even a whisper in Stratford as to how, during those years, he turned to poetry and playwriting and rose to competency in both.* If in

* We are justified in assuming that by the age of eighteen William Shakespeare had passed beyond such dabbling in verse as four lines which the countryfolk of eight villages in Warwickshire ascribe to him, lines which they say he composed during a carouse at the Falcon Inn at Bidford, after which he and his companions slept out the night under a crabapple tree. Those lines are in tourist guidebooks where they belong.

Stratford there had been an exemplar, teacher, or patron who influenced and encouraged the town hero in verse writing, Stratford folk would surely have retained some proud remembrance of him. It seems reasonably certain that his native town would have a tradition of such a teacher or patron had Shakespeare resided there during those years. The absence of such a tradition makes it seem more than likely that he spent those years elsewhere. In this supremely consequential matter, Stratford-upon-Avon is an absolute vacuum.

Young Will Shakespeare had good reason to get away from Stratford. It would have been advisable for him to put distance between himself and the cloud which enveloped the family, and to attempt to climb without the incubus of his father's recusancy and suspected Papistry.

If he left Stratford "with a band of strolling players,"[9] but had no acting experience, how could he have paid his way? There seems to be no evidence that he was adept at playing any musical instrument, although Louis C. Elson shows that Shakespeare was undoubtedly a capable singer and dancer.[10] Being young enough to participate in sports, however, he may have earned his way as an acrobat. The "Accounts of the Revels" suggest the possibility: "Sundry feates of Tumbling, and activity, were showed before her Majestie on New yeares day at night by the Lord Strange his servants." Alan Keen and Roger Lubbock tell us that "Lord Strange's Company between 1580 and 1587 was merely a troupe of acrobats or tumblers composed of boys or youths."[11]

In what shire of England would Shakespeare most likely have sought livelihood with an acting company in his pre-London years? Alan Keen cites evidences that he visited Shropshire at some time during his life, but these give no indication as to whether it was before or after he went to London. Shakespeare shows intimate knowledge of Shropshire, particularly the Severn River near Eyton, where the stream was, as he called it, "sandy-bottom'd,"* but other Shropshire evidences are few. There are, however, varied and impressive evidences that he spent much time in Lancashire during his pre-London years.[12] These, plus the new evidences presented in the following three chapters, may not add up to proof, but they do point to the most reasonable theory, a theory which is gathering strength.

* Local fishermen near Eyton can direct one to the "sandy-bottom'd" area.

If upon leaving Stratford Will Shakespeare carried a letter of recommendation, it most naturally would have been one procured from the Master of Stratford Grammar School. John Cottam, the Master from 1579 until he was sent to the Tower in 1582, was a man with Papist sympathies. A recommendation by Cottam would most likely have been addressed to someone in Lancashire, the shire from which he himself had come.

4

SHAKESHAFTE

"What's in a name?"

ROMEO AND JULIET, 2.2.43

Sir EDMUND CHAMBERS SAYS OF YOUNG WILLIAM Shakespeare: "It is possible that he is to be identified with a William Shakeshafte, who in 1581 was a player in a company mentioned by one Alexander Houghton [in his will] of Lea in Lancashire."[1]

"Possible . . . to be identified" skirts the fact that "Shakespeare" and "Shakeshafte" were the same name. Three years before William Shakespeare was born, his presumed grandfather, Richard, signed himself "Shakeshafte," and also answered to "Shakestaff." These were the same name in alternative forms. Shaft, Staff, and Spear were accepted variations because they bore the same meaning. Names were not fully crystallized in the sixteenth century. The only form of the name used in Lancashire was Shakeshafte. The parish records of Lancashire show several Shakeshaftes, but no William

Shakeshafte born there who would have been young in 1581. Considering the extreme unlikelihood of there having been two youths of the same but not very common name, both just at the age to become apprentices, and both of them players, it is more than probable that young William Shakespeare was the actor mentioned in Alexander Houghton's will.

Here is part of the text of that will in its original spelling:

> It ys my wyll that Thos. Houghton of Bryne-Scoules my brother shall have all my instruments belonginge to mew sycke and all man^r of playclothes yf he be minded to keepe and do keppe players. And yf he wyll not keppe and mantayne players than it is my wyll that Sr. Thomas Heskethe, Knyghte, shall have the same instruments and playe clothes and I most hertelye requyre the said Sr. Thomas to be ffrendlye unto ffoke Gyllome* and Willm Shakeshafte, now dwelling with me. And ether take theym unto his servyce or else helpe theym to some mr.

That last request with use of "mr." (master) is a clear implication that the two young players were of an age to become apprentices. Since the term of a statutory appenticeship in Elizabethan times was seven years, and since apprentices were compelled by statute to be twenty-four years of age before coming out of their apprenticeship, the presumption is strong that in 1581 Gyllome and Shakeshafte were seventeen years old.

Further provisions in the will were that the rent from lands in Wythnell "shalbe devydette amongste" eleven named beneficiaries as annuities "during theyr naturall lyves. The porcon of that partye that shll dye shalbe equallye devyded amongste theym that shall survyve soe that the survyvor of them all shall have for his lyffe the said whole rents of syxtyne pounds thryttyne shillings foure pence." The annuities for two of the beneficiaries were "unto ffowke Gyllom fortye shyllings unto Willm Shakeshafte ffortye shyllings."

The immediate effect of receiving the precise sum of forty shillings was to give the young men a significant legal and economic status. Early in Queen Elizabeth's reign "it had been enacted that

---

* The name Gyllome (Gwillim, Gwilym, Guillim, Gillum) does not appear elsewhere in Lancashire records. The name is common in Monmouthshire and Herefordshire, and it exists in Northumberland. It was probably Welsh.

every unmarried person between the ages of twelve and sixty, and every married person under thirty, who possessed less than forty shillings a year should work as a servant hired by the year." The legacy of forty shillings per annum freed Shakeshafte from the necessity of hiring out as a servant, or of laboring as a farm hand.

It has been assumed that upon the death of Alexander Houghton, that same year (1581), Shakeshafte and Gyllome entered the service of Sir Thomas Hesketh. But in his will Houghton had said that the play clothes should go to Sir Thomas Hesketh only if his brother Thomas Houghton did not decide to keep players. The two young actors were already in the household at Lea Hall where they may have remained under Thomas. Thomas Houghton had a larger hall in another manor house, Hoghton Tower, where there were "revels, masques, and dances." Because he had many children, at least ten by 1581, his wife and children would have wished him to keep players. Alexander Houghton's will makes it seem probable that the question as to keeping players was being debated in Thomas Houghton's household. Thomas Houghton in his will, made in 1588, does not specify players, and mentions only "children, servants, tenants, and other persons," but both "servants" and "other persons" may have included players. We know that Sir Thomas Hesketh did keep players, and was "a notable great householder and benefactor to all men singular in every science."

To which of the two households Gyllome and Shakeshafte went would seem to make little difference biographically. Hesketh Hall at Rufford was only twelve miles from Hoghton Tower, the principal seat of Thomas Houghton. The Hesketh and Houghton families had several houses in the same region, and were much intermarried, each with many children. Sir Thomas Hesketh was by marriage related to the Stanley family, Lord Strange's, whose Lathom House was only four miles from Rufford, and whose New Park was not far either. Lord Strange later became the Earl of Derby. The seat of the earl, Knowsley, was eight miles south of Lathom House. Players retained at any of the manor houses in that part of Lancashire would have been seen and known in all the other houses.

Alexander Houghton's concern for the future of the two young players evinces an exceptional sense of responsibility toward them. His leaving them legacies just large enough to insure them against

23

ever being forced into manual labor argues that he perceived in them some unique talent quite beyond the ordinary. It was presumably more than an ability as actors, since if they showed great promise as actors, their future would take care of itself. The talent he saw in them was more likely of a kind that needed some special nurture to be brought to flower. Poetic ability was the talent which above all others would have commended them to the Lancashire gentry in the orbit of Ferdinando Stanley, Lord Strange, who was a patron and friend of many poets and himself an ardent verse writer. It is a reasonable guess that young Gyllome and Shakeshafte had revealed unusual ability in verse writing.

The annuity may have been a factor in Will Shakespeare's betrothal the following summer, when he was only eighteen. His marriage grew out of what was probably a vacation romance. Modern prurience, ignorant of old customs, has stressed the fact that Shakespeare's first child was born five and one-half months after he went through the legal formalities that opened the way for his marriage. Some have assumed that his was a shotgun wedding.

In Elizabethan times there were two church ceremonies before a couple became man and wife. The first was betrothal, the second, a wedding. The betrothal was the more sensitive of the ceremonies, more immediate to the natural discovery of love. To many minds it was the more significant. It was spiritually binding, though not indissoluble under church law. Whether or not a couple had found their love by sleeping together, a public betrothal testified to the man's honorable intentions. A betrothal came when it was called for. A wedding, on the other hand, often required much time to prepare, what with sending invitations to those who might reside at a distance and who would have to make plans in advance for attending it.

In the absence of most of the records, one simply cannot say that Will Shakespeare and Anne Hathaway were not religiously betrothed in the summer of 1582, with the approval of their parents.

In the Register at Worcester on November 27 there is this Entry of License for Marriage: "Willelmum Shaxpere et Annam Whatley de Temple Grafton," and on the next day there is the record of a bond of Sureties in the large amount of £40 (equivalent to $5,000) given by friends of "William Shagspere" for his marriage to "Anne Hathway of Stratford." Scandal lovers exclaim: Two

24

girls! One the beloved, whom he wished to marry, but twenty-four hours later he was forced to agree to marry the other!

Not so. The clerk who wrote "Whatley" when he should have written "Hathway" may have been deaf, or befuddled with ale, or he may have inadvertently written "Whatley" because on the very same day there had been a suit involving a William Whatley. No Anne Whatley of Temple Grafton has ever been found. The clerk would not likely have muddled Temple Grafton with Stratford, unless that confusion was deliberate (there may have been intention of having a Catholic ceremony); or unless Anne Hathaway may at the time have been staying with relatives in Temple Grafton while her legal residence was in or near Stratford, in which case there only appears to have been confusion where actually there was none.

The Bond of Sureties, required since Will Shakespeare was a minor, gave guarantee that there was no legal impediment or no suit alleging an impediment to the marriage; that he would not proceed without the consent of the bride's parents; and that his friends would reimburse the Bishop of Worcester for any fine the bishop might have to pay for issuing the license. This was a normal procedure when a marriage was to be expedited with the issuing of a special license which required only a single proclaiming of banns.

The wish to avoid a delay of an additional two proclaimings of banns was significant in a record dated November 28, for just ahead was a prohibited six weeks' period from December 2 to January 13 during which no banns could be proclaimed. Without the special license, Will Shakespeare and Anne Hathaway would have had to wait until the final two banns had been proclaimed on the first two Sundays after January 13.

There was patently a desire for speed. But it must have been something other than a pregnancy of only three and one-half months that necessitated such haste. Even if Anne and Will had mistakenly believed that the pregnancy had begun a month earlier than it actually had, a marriage at the end of January would have come long before their child was born.

The desire to avoid delay therefore had some other cause. The most likely explanation is that Will Shakespeare had commitments which would require his presence at some considerable distance from Stratford in January and for several months thereafter.

25

Anne Hathaway was twenty-six when she married the eighteen-year-old Will Shakespeare. The disparity in their ages suggests that he found in her more intellectual companionship than in any of the girls he had met of his own age, and that Will was brought to the altar at least in part by the dictates of his poetic temperament, and not merely by charm, unless, of course, one insists upon thinking him a victim.

5

FORTUNATE YEARS
1581-1587

"Fortune and I are friends."

TROILUS AND CRESSIDA, 3.3.88

W<small>E HAVE SEEN WHY IT WAS EXPEDIENT FOR YOUNG</small> Shakespeare to get away from Stratford in 1581. He had far more urgent reason for being somewhere else in 1583, after a conspiracy of Papists was uncovered among his mother's relatives. John Somerville, husband of Margaret Arden of Park Hall, who was a cousin of Shakespeare's mother, set out on October 25 to shoot Queen Elizabeth, but was intercepted. Investigation revealed that he had been incited by the Park Hall priest Hugh Hall, and Margaret Arden and her father Edward Arden shared guilty knowledge of the plot. All three were arrested and taken to London with Somerville. The four were tried, convicted, and sentenced, the men to be hanged, drawn, and quartered, and Margaret Arden to be burned at the stake.[1] Suspicion extended the investigation to Stratford, with extreme peril to Shakespeare's parents.

The Government desired to find proof of a far-reaching plot behind this act of individual madness and Walsingham sent strict injunctions to Stratford that more victims must be found and further evidence uncovered. . . . Thomas Wilkes replied [from Stratford] to Walsingham suggesting he make the prisoners speak through torture. . . . "The Warwickshire recusants sustain each other. Unless you can charge them with matter from the mouths of your prisoners, look not to wring anything from them here." Walsingham dealt with the case in a different manner. Somerville instead of being led out to execution where the appearance of a raving madman would have caused scandal and defeated the political purpose of the execution was strangled in prison and the government declared that this horrid crime had been perpetrated by his fellow-plotters lest he betray the names of all those who were engaged with him to kill the Queen. . . . Mrs. Stopes supposes Father Hall to have died under question [torture] as after his last examination all trace of him is lost. [2]

The Ardens were executed on December 20, 1583. "The outrage and the penalties brought disgrace to her [Shakespeare's mother's] family. Her husband's troubles were petty compared with this."[3]

Anti-Catholic sentiment ran high and continued to rise, until allayed by the defeat of the Spanish Armada. Shakespeare's parents were lucky in that they were never arrested as recusants or Papists. John Shakespeare seems to have been adroit in disposing of enough of his visible property among his trusted friends so that it could not be confiscated if he were condemned, and he himself would not appear to be worth capturing. The fanatics were greedy. There is no conclusive evidence that he was in financial straits. Almost certainly the contrary. "Only after ten years' persistent non-attendance was his name removed from the list of aldermen,"[4] though it likely would have been immediately removed had he suffered the financial reverses some have supposed.

Stratford was a dangerous place for a lad whose parents were under suspicion. Will Shakespeare showed no inclination toward martyrdom.

There is a well-grounded tradition that Shakespeare was "in his younger years a schoolteacher in the country." This was said about 1680 by John Aubrey who says he got it "from Mr. Beeston," who probably was William Beeston, Governor of a company of actors in 1640. For teaching school, an "usher" would have received about £10 a year. It is questionable, however, whether the son of a suspected recusant would have been given employment in any church-controlled school. It is more likely that, if he was a teacher, it was as tutor in a manor house, instructing the children of nobles or gentry. What he would have been paid as tutor would not have fed five mouths: his wife's, his children's, and his own. His daughter Susanna had been born in 1583, and the twins Hamnet and Judith in January 1584. He would necessarily have supplemented his income by other work during vacations.

The breadth of view Shakespeare acquired during his pre-London years would seem to indicate that for most of those years he had a horizon wider than the walls of a schoolroom. *Love's Labour's Lost* shows that its author was a foe to pedantry.

Clues to the scenery in the region where Shakespeare spent at least some of his pre-London years are the figures of speech in his writings dealing with a geographical feature—mountains. They all point in one direction of the compass in relation to that feature. In *Shakespeare's Imagery and What It Tells Us*, Caroline Spurgeon did not include the word "mountains," probably for the reason that the poet's use of the word in all but two or three instances lacks poetic vividness. For example, he has "mountain lioness" in *Titus Andronicus*; "Strong-fixed is the house of Lancaster and like a mountain" in *Henry VI, Part 3*; "barren mountains," "gross as a mountain, open palpable," and "goats ran from the mountains" in *Henry IV, Part 1*; "rocky mountains" in *Henry IV, Part 2*; "white his shroud as the mountain snow" in *Hamlet*; "forked mountain or blue promontory" in *Antony and Cleopatra*; "as the rudest wind, that by the top doth take the mountain pine" in *Cymbeline*; "turfy mountains where live nibbling sheep" in *The Tempest*; and "mountain cedar" in *Henry VIII*. None of these is indicative of close familiarity with mountains, beyond what their author might have learned from reading or from a picture showing mountains in the background. Slightly more suggestive of his actually having seen mountains are these words: "small and indistinguishable, like far-off mountains turned into clouds" in *Midsummer Night's Dream*. But here also there is no sense of close familiarity, and very definitely the contrary.

On the other hand, there are three references to mountains, two of them vivid poetic figures, which make us feel that they stem from an actual viewing of mountains:

29

In *Hamlet*, 4.1.29, we have: "The sun no sooner shall the mountains touch," the context of which shows it to be a reference to early morning. This line does not describe mountains to the east of the beholder, from behind which the sun rises, but mountains to the west touched by the glow of color from the light cast upon them by the rising sun. The plural indicates a range or group of mountains seen from a distance, instead of one mountain seen close up.

In Sonnet 33, one of the supremely great poetic figures is this:

> Full many a glorious morning have I seen
> Flatter the mountain-tops with sovereign eye.

Here again Shakespeare clearly has a mental picture of mountains to the west of him, and of plural mountains, which he has seen gilded with early sunlight on many mornings. We must remember, of course, that Europeans, quite contrary to the Chinese, apparently did not develop a love for mountain scenery until long after Shakespeare's time, and hence his apt word "flatter" is suggestive of a lack of beauty in mountains, and helps explain the scarcity of his poetical references to them.

The same compass direction and the same coloring from the rising sun are indicated in *Romeo and Juliet* by another of Shakespeare's great poetic figures, which also refers to plural mountains:

> Jocund day
> Stands tiptoe on the misty mountain tops.

If imagery warrants any biographical assumption, the figures of speech relating to mountains give several new hints:

1. Shakespeare saw mountains, but never intimately, and only from a distance. If he had seen mountains close up or had negotiated a mountain pass, he would have been impressed with some awesome height or roaring cataract or frightening cliff, an animal poised on a dizzy crag or leaping over a crevasse, and in his imagery we might expect to find at least one vivid figure of some such impression. From the absence of any such, it seems reasonable to assume that he never got near mountains.

2. Shakespeare saw mountains in the distance only from the east of them, the mountains being far off to the west of him.

3. Sonnet 33 gives evidence that the figure of speech in it was conceived from the poet's memory of a place where there was a view of distant mountains to the west. This place was not Stratford and not London. It was not in the eastern half of England, but somewhere in the western half of the country.

In Lancashire, the ancestral home of the Houghton family, Hoghton Tower, is on a hill of 556 feet elevation. Only low ground, Houghton Bottom, and so forth, lies between it and the seacoast. From the hill on which Hoghton Tower stands, there is a view westward which includes the peaks of the English Lake District and the far-off mountains of North Wales.

The gentry in Lancashire were notably hospitable to poets and actors. Lancashire would have beckoned to young Shakespeare most strongly, for in all England outside of London, the greatest concentration of interest in the presentation of plays was in that shire. Plays were given not only in the manor houses of Lathom, Rufford, Knowsley, New Park, Hawthorpe, Dunkenhalge, and others, but Lancashire had a public playhouse at Prescot, two and one-half miles from Knowsley. The site of the Prescot Playhouse is within the present city of Liverpool.

An oral tradition places young Shakespeare in Rufford at the Old Hall, but since we do not know when that tradition began, no credence can be placed upon it. It may have been initiated by Lancashire theories published by Keen and Lubbock in 1951 and 1954. The occupants of Lea manor house were saying in 1962 that Shakespeare in his youth spent two years at Lea, but their "tradition" could have been an echo of the "Shakeshafte" evidence in Alexander Houghton's will. As to a statement emanating from Rufford, "A neighbouring solicitor recalls seeing some documents in which the name Shakeshafte was changed to Shakespeare,"[5] there is no certainty that it refers to our poet. A more definite hint of a connection with Rufford is that years later in London in a business deal, Shakespeare chose as a fellow trustee a friend of his, Thomas Savage, who was born in Rufford. Another possible connection with Rufford is that if Shakespeare was employed there as tutor or player, he would have met there John Salisbury who was lauded in Robert Chester's *Love's Martyr*, a volume in which Shakespeare's *The Phoenix and the Turtle* was also published.

31

LIKE TO THE LARK

There is more definite evidence which seems to link Shakespeare with Lathom Hall, less than a half hour's horseback ride from Rufford. In Lathom Hall there was a great screen painted with signs of the Zodiac, over which Lord Strange's players shot arrows bearing letters.[6] In *Titus Andronicus*, 4.3.48–68, Marcus and Titus and others "in a public place" shoot "arrows with letters on the ends of them" as petitions to the gods for Justice. They say one arrow landed "in Virgo's lap," another broke off "one of Taurus' horns," and another "gave Aries such a knock that down fell both the Ram's horns in the Court." So it seems very probable that Shakespeare was familiar with Lathom Hall.

A connection between players licensed by Lancashire noblemen and Shakespeare's acting company in London is shown by Keen and Lubbock. In 1581 the will of Alexander Houghton of Lea named the young player William Shakeshafte and commended him to Thomas Houghton and/or to Sir Thomas Hesketh of Rufford. In 1587, "Sir Thomas Hesketh's plaiers went awaie" (Official Household Records of the Stanleys). They probably joined Lord Strange's Men. The Earl of Leicester's Men visited the Earl of Derby in Lancashire. The next year, Lord Strange's Men and the Earl of Leicester's Men merged into one acting company. Later, Lord Strange's Men merged with the Queen's Players. Shakespeare may have been with the Queen's Players who acted in Lancashire in 1588. In 1589, Shakespeare may have been at Knowsley in June. Lord Strange's Men were at least part of the time in London. In 1591, they were in possession of the Rose Theatre. In 1592, Ferdinando Stanley, Lord Strange, became Earl of Derby. In April 1594, the earl died and Lord Strange's Men passed to Ferdinando Stanley's brother-in-law, George Carey, the first Lord Hunsdon, Lord Chamberlain. William Shakespeare was with this acting company by that time. The above facts suggest a tie between Shakespeare and Lancashire.

Further, Keen and Lubbock in *The Annotator* argue that marginal notes in a copy of Hall's *Chronicle*, which in all probability had been in Lancashire, could be and probably are in Shakespeare's handwriting. S. M. Pitcher thinks it likely that Shakespeare made these notes in preparation for writing *The Famous Victories* in 1586.

The leading persons in Elizabethan times were receptive to poetry to a degree that seems unbelievable in our more scientific age. Verse writing was practiced by courtiers and noblemen, and, indeed, by any man who had pretensions to culture. It was a greatly admired and cherished talent. *Venus and Adonis* inevitably aroused the enthusiasm of any who were privileged to read it in manuscript. *Henry VI, Part 3* and *The Comedy of Errors* were impressive as beginner's works. When a young man revealed such talent, it would have been quite within the manners of the time for some nobleman to commission an artist to paint the young man's portrait. It is entirely credible that Shakespeare was honored by having his portrait painted as early as 1588.

In the John Rylands Library in Manchester there is a portrait of a young man with this inscription: "aetatis suae 24–1588." This so-called Grafton Portrait was unquestionably painted in the Elizabethan period. Announcement of its discovery was in the *Manchester Guardian* on February 18, 1907. A clue as to where it may have been painted possibly lies in the fact that a portrait of Ferdinando Stanley painted at Knowsley has a collar like the one in the Grafton portrait.*

If it is a portrait of Shakespeare and had been in his possession, it is easy to see how it got to Northamptonshire, to Grafton Regis, from which it takes its name. Shakespeare's granddaughter, Elizabeth Hall, who fell heir to Shakespeare's estate when her husband Thomas Nash died, married John Bernard of Abbington Abbey, moved there in 1653, and died there in 1670. Abbington Abbey or Manor is only eight miles from Grafton Regis. The age of twenty-four in 1588 does not fit any of the men of the Stanley family in Lancashire or in Grafton Regis, so far as existing records show.

Annie Doris Wraight attempts to convince her readers that the Grafton is a portrait of the same young man shown in a Cambridge portrait whom she believes to be Christopher Marlowe. In trying to force a comparison, she ignores obvious differences in features. She does, however, state that the "Marlowe" eyes are "quite dark, definitely brown," and those in the Grafton are "slate grey." To build her argument that no portrait of Shakespeare would have been painted in oils as early as 1588, she says: "At that time Shakespeare was quite unknown. . . . Marlowe, on the other hand, was an M.A. [Master of Art] and a famous playwright [and] had undoubtedly acquired wealthy patronage."[7] Our new knowledge of what

---

* The portrait of Ferdinando Stanley is now in the possession of Mr. Eric E. Porter, Horton Court, Chipping Sodbury, Gloucestershire.

33

Shakespeare wrote during his pre-London years challenges precisely this and many other preconceptions.

The Grafton picture is $17\frac{1}{2}'' \times 15''$ on a panel of oak. The painting is in bad condition, with pitted holes and scars. The young man has dark brown hair, in the present state of the pigments. He has sensuous lips, with the middle lobe of the upper lip drawn down into firmness. This pronounced dip of the middle lobe of the upper lip is a feature of many Shakespeare portraits painted years after his death: the Droeshout, Flower, Janssen, Ashbourne, Stratford, and so forth.

No highlight comparable to that on the forehead now appears on the nose in the Grafton Portrait, although the quality of the painting makes it reasonable to assume that the artist originally gave the nose a proper lighting. The enlarged end of the nose, incompatible with the sharp nasal ridge, is clearly the result of botched retouching. Thomas Kay says: "A very slight touch of light upon the nasal column to replace that which is lost affords a rather exaggerated but effectual restoration."[8]

The young man of the Grafton Portrait has eyes that are keenly observant, reflective, and introspective. He is under tension of an inner vision, with a leanness suggestive of great effort and a determination stronger than any disillusionment. Since it is probably a portrait of Shakespeare just before the beginning of his London career, we may apply to it the words in *Titus Andronicus* (4.2.108), written the year after the portrait was painted:

> This myself;
> The vigour and the picture of my youth.

More convincing evidence than any hitherto advanced for believing that the Grafton is a portrait of Shakespeare is in the following chain of facts:

The so-called Darmstadt Death-Mask has been established beyond question as that of William Shakespeare of Stratford.[9]

The man who is checkmating Ben Jonson in the Chess Picture by Karel van Mander in 1604, and who is identified in numerous ways as Shakespeare (see Chapter 15), shortly after he had written *Hamlet*, has features identical with those of the Death-Mask seen in the same three-quarter profile.

34

The "Grafton" Portrait, 1588

The Shakespeare Death-Mask in three-quarter profile

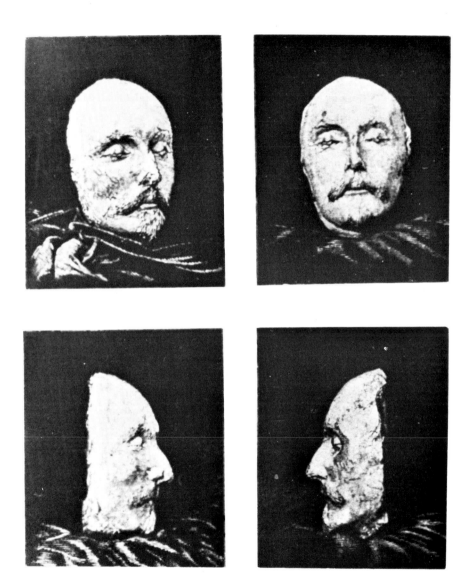

Four views of the Shakespeare Death-Mask

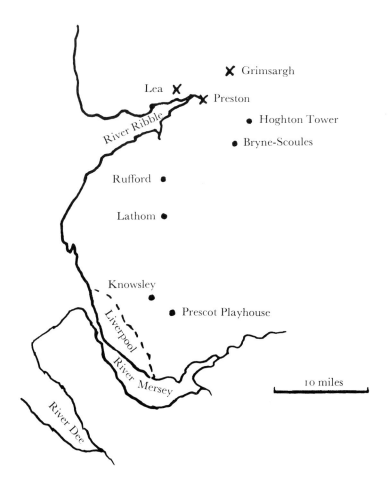

Lancashire manor houses
where plays were performed

The Grafton Portrait shows a youth with the same facial structure as the Death-Mask and the man on the right in the Chess Picture.

Thus far we have a dozen Lancashire evidences. That there are so many would seem to be by more than mere chance. We are not only justified but are practically compelled to extend hospitality toward the belief that Lancashire was the shire in which Shakespeare spent his pre-London years.

The nature of the experiences he had during those years are most certainly such as are hinted at through the dozen evidences. Wherever he was, he became acquainted with the manners and customs of gentlemen—their habits, quirks, and sports. He had contacts with noble families, and if the term will not be misunderstood, he was exposed to spiritual aristocracy, or to persons who in their day were held to be aristocrats in behavior. In other words, he had an opportunity to observe closely the characteristics of nobles who plotted and counterplotted in a hotbed of ambition, intrigue, and betrayal, such as existed in Lancashire and such as he portrayed in *Henry VI, Part 3*.*

During his pre-London years Shakespeare became saturated with a feudal atmosphere and code, and acquired lasting respect for legal authority in its maintenance of the political stability of the nation. He learned the value of a justice not too emasculated by soft-hearted sentiment. He had convenient access to books, and sufficient leisure, we deduce, to develop the habit of literary productiveness.

He did not waste his time during the years 1581 to 1587. By or before 1588 he passed beyond being merely a facile versifier, for he had written not only a sensationally appealing narrative poem, but at least two plays, which in all probability had been performed on the road and in some manor houses.† In the face of this new knowledge we can no longer call the pre-London years the Blank Years or the

---

* Ferdinando Stanley, Lord Strange, who became Earl of Derby, was the legitimate heir to the throne, after the Queen herself. His mother was a granddaughter of King Henry VIII's sister. He was a Catholic, and the Catholics pinned their hopes on him, but when the machinations of his enthusiasts brought their treasonable plans into the open, he repudiated them and denounced Sir Thomas Hesketh, who, as his scapegoat, was executed in November 1588.

† In *Brief Lives*, written during the second half of the seventeenth century, John Aubrey's statement regarding Shakespeare—"He began to make eassays at Dramatique Poetry"—may have referred to pre-London writings.

Lost Years. Those years were not blank or lost to the poet, and they are no longer entirely blank or lost to us. Because of the growth we know Shakespeare achieved during those years, we now can call them the Full Years, or the Fortunate Years.

What seems to be a more compelling evidence for Lancashire than any yet presented is the discovery that the young man who inspired Shakespeare's sonnets to his friend was a Lancashire youth. This discovery is presented in Chapter 14, "The Planted Name."

6

YOUNG LOVE

"Age, I do abhor thee, youth, I do adore thee;
O, my love, my love is young!"

THE PASSIONATE PILGRIM, 12.9–10

"In particular, a writer's early work often reflects his personal experience."[1] In *Literary Biography* Leon Edel says: "A writer's first words are generally his most transparently autobiographical. . . . Contrary to general opinion, Shakespeare is an intensely autobiographical writer in his non-dramatic writings." This is certainly true. And, it is just as true that he is rarely autobiographical in his plays.

The findings in Appendix A show that the earliest written of all Shakespeare's published works is the miscellaneous group of poems called *The Passionate Pilgrim.** In these poems we hear the first singing of the lark. These poems, with the possible exception of the first two, were composed soon after their author's marriage.

---

* It will not be pedantic to cite here the definition of "pilgrim" (in *Webster's Third New International*) as "a person who passes through life as if in exile from a heavenly homeland or in search of it or of some high goal (as truth)."

37

The Passionate Pilgrim poems show features of recognizable Shakespearean style. They are beginner's work, but they have some lines so neatly turned and some so consecutively felicitous that they appear to be distillations of much practice verse, by one who has acquired considerable skill in his devotion to the writing of poetry.

Hasty assumptions regarding the authorship of these poems have led to a belief among some scholars that the majority of them are of doubtful ascription. This is simply not so. Here are the facts:

The Passionate Pilgrim collection consists of fourteen sonnets and poems.* Of these, Nos. 1 and 2 are inferior and early versions of Shakespeare's Sonnets 138 and 144. Nos. 3 and 5 appear in *Love's Labour's Lost*. No. 12 is found in several dramatists' works, for it is so good that several borrowed it, but as George Lyman Kittredge says, it is "usually accepted as Shakespeare's."[2] Eleven of the fourteen poems are found only in Shakespeare. Nos. 8 and 11 are the only poems among the fourteen whose authorship has been called into question by their printing history.

Poem No. 8, a sonnet, was first printed by John Jaggard in 1598 as Richard Barnfield's, but the printer's brother William Jaggard the next year published it in *The Passionate Pilgrim* as Shakespeare's. William Jaggard subsequently omitted it from his next edition (1605?) of poems by Barnfield. The evidence seems clear that in the informed opinion of the Jaggards Shakespeare wrote it. Further, it was not included among Barnfield's collected sonnets, in all of which the meter, vocabulary, and manner mark them as not by Shakespeare. None of Barnfield's sonnets would be mistaken for Shakespeare's by anyone familiar with Shakespeare's style. No. 8 of *The Passionate Pilgrim* in every particular could be Shakespeare's. In absence of any proof to the contrary, it is reasonable to accept the poem as Shakespeare's.

The first ten lines of *The Passionate Pilgrim* No. 11 were printed in Bartholomew Griffin's *Fidessa* in 1596, but it has been suspected that several poems in that volume were not by Griffin. The last four lines

* In the same volume with *The Passionate Pilgrim*, six other poems were printed after a separate title which does not claim the six for Shakespeare. "Only on close inspection would the purchasers discover that merely the first section actually was attributed to the master."[3] Of those six other poems, considering them as numbered 15 to 20, Shakespeare has No. 16 in *Love's Labour's Lost* (4.3.101) and Kittredge says No. 18 may be Shakespeare's. None of these six other poems, however, is included in our discussion.

of No. 11 first appeared when that poem was printed in *The Passionate Pilgrim* (1599) as Shakespeare's.

Since the printing histories of Nos. 8 and 11 strongly favor their being accepted as Shakespeare's, there is no reason to surrender any of the fourteen poems of *The Passionate Pilgrim*.

Except for the first two sonnets, which patently refer to the poet's mistress and friend, *The Passionate Pilgrim* poems were written early enough for us to say that Shakespeare's marriage was the principal romantic experience he had before he wrote them. His marriage directly enters into the subject matter of several of these poems. Poem No. 10, however, tells us that a girl friend of the poet had died: "Sweet rose, fair flower, untimely pluck'd, . . . kill'd too soon by death's sharp sting, . . . Thy discontent thou didst bequeath to me." And in poem No. 14 (in the Craig edition), the poet laments his parting from his "pretty" as he goes into his "exile," though he may "wander" back, "wander" being "a word for shadows like myself, as take the pain, but cannot pluck the pelf."

It is biographically suggestive that in some of *The Passionate Pilgrim* poems the female was the active agent, while Adonis "rose and ran away." Adonis "stood stark naked on the brook's green brim," but as soon as he spied Cytherea, he "bounc'd in" under the water. When the Queen of Love warned him against being wounded in the thigh by a boar, and to emphasize the warning, showed him her own thigh, Adonis "blushing fled." The young poet was interested in the situation of a reluctant male.

Shakespeare's marrying at eighteen implies that he was normally heterosexual. But his early poetry shows there was another tendency in him. The sonnets reveal his coming into full awareness of it. Leslie A. Fiedler says: "There is only one major theme of the Sonnets unexpressed in *The Passionate Pilgrim* and this is the notion of the Two Immortalities which underlies that of the Two Loves."[4] Several of *The Passionate Pilgrim* poems are concerned with the pains of adjustment in love. For example, we have in poem No. 7:

> She burn'd with love, as straw with fire flameth;
> She burn'd out love, as soon as straw out-burneth;
> She framed the love, and yet she foil'd the framing;
> She bade love last, and yet she fell a-turning.
> Was this a lover, or a lecher whether?

The poet here holds the concept that in mating the female should be subordinate. It seems unavoidable to conclude that Shakespeare at the time of his marriage, or soon after, felt sex to be alarming. He may have feared it as a breaking down of the tension he found essential to sustained poetic creativity.

If No. 8 of *The Passionate Pilgrim* is Shakespeare's, as we have full reason to believe, it merits special attention as containing Shakespeare's only mention by name of any of his poet contemporaries.* While this would make it of large significance biographically, nevertheless such a personal literary criticism was from the point of view of Shakespeare in his maturity a reason for discarding the poem as an "unconsidered trifle," since in being concerned with named persons, it falls short of universal applicability.

Poem No. 8 would testify to the sensitivity of young Shakespeare in that his unique voicing of a direct literary judgment was called forth by the greatest of his poet contemporaries. However it may be, Shakespeare was not interested in literature to the extent most lovers of the bard might suppose. Or better said, he was more interested in life than in anything written about life. Yet the critical estimate of Edmund Spenser—"whose deep conceit is such as passing all conceit, needs no defence"—is a most discerning comment on that poet. It is perceptive enough to sound like a statement by Shakespeare. In keeping with his love of song and his own limited formal education, Shakespeare would naturally have been less impressed with Spenser's classical learning than with his lyricism.

The "singing" of Spenser referred to in No. 8 of *The Passionate Pilgrim* is the singing in *The Shepherd's Calendar*, printed in 1579, and again in 1581. Singing by "the shepheards boye" or by Hobinoll or Colin occurs extensively in six of the eclogues, those for January, April, June, August, November, and December. Spenser himself felt he might need defense. *The Shepherd's Calendar* contained matter that could be perilous to its author, for it repudiated all three groups of religionists in England: Romanists, Anglicans, and Puritans. The eclogue for May presented the daring argument that the reasoning of both Catholics and Protestants made it dangerous to reveal fellowship with either. Although Spenser had reason to fear the authorities, he had the support of politically influential

40   *   With the exception of a pun on Greene in Sonnet 112.

friends, and was unmolested. The poem was published anonymously. It was the custom among gentlemen to "publish" by privately distributing manuscript copies. For example, when Spenser's *Hymns to Love and to Beauty* were first printed in 1596, their author wrote of them: "Having in the greener time of my youth [about 1575] composed these former two hymns . . . I was moved . . . to call in the same. But being unable so to doe, by reason that many copies were formerly scattered abroad . . . "

The printed *Shepherd's Calendar* had the attraction of professed anonymity of authorship, but the name of its author was an open secret among those who had read it in manuscript. William Webbe identified its author as "Master Sp."[5] Shakespeare, it appears, was ecstatic over Spenser's poetry and especially his "singing."

In his own singing, our ambitious young poet no doubt desired to emulate and maybe surpass Spenser.

The knowledge that *Venus and Adonis* was composed six or seven years earlier than has hitherto been accepted, gives that poem a biographical significance it would not otherwise have. If it had been a work tossed off by an already successful dramatist as a side issue to pleasure a patron, its contents would not have such significance. But as the first extensive work undertaken by a young poet, it brings to focus his choice of theme, the theme of a reluctant male. Some will ask: Why assume that Adonis reflects the personality of the poet any more than Tarquin does in *The Rape of Lucrece*? Our answer is that the presence of that same neurotic Adonis theme in *The Passionate Pilgrim* makes it seem more than likely that *Venus and Adonis* does mirror its youthful author's personal reactions.*

Venus and Adonis dealt daringly with sex. Circulated in manuscript among nobles and gentry, it was certain to mark its author in their minds as a youth of exceptional promise, a poet who could write sensationally, yet who was clever enough to avoid the shame of indecency. He was obviously a youth for whose future achievement as a poet there could be the highest hopes. He was deserving of financial assistance, the more since his luscious narrative poem

---

* Robert Adger Law thinks *Venus and Adonis* "owes much to Lodge's *Scillaes Metamorphosis* (1589)."[6] There seems to be very little parallel, if any. Because of what we now know as to the dating, if there was indebtedness in either direction, the borrowing must have been by Lodge after reading *Venus and Adonis* in manuscript.

41

showed vigorous enthusiasm for horses and a keen love of gentle-men's sports: the unforgettable description of a hare hunt, the manly lust for boar-hunting, the full-blooded activity of a stallion with a mare. The poem could not fail to delight all Englishmen who loved horses. It was a sure patronage winner, and no doubt reaped its author immediate rewards, but we now know that Shakespeare held it for about seven years until he found a patron to whom he wished to dedicate its printing (see Appendix A).

7

SHAKESPEARE'S
"ART"

*"had I but the means
To hold a rival place with one of them."*

MERCHANT OF VENICE, 1.1.174

As YOUNG WILL SHAKESPEARE RODE HIS HORSE TOWARD London, ambition surged in his breast. Sonnets 50 and 51 give evidence of his mode of traveling. That ambition surged in his breast is supposition, but there is no acceptable alternative.

One of the plays in his saddlebags was *Henry VI, Part 3*. It was his first play, unless *The Famous Victories*, a chronicle history in prose, was an earlier work of his. The subject matter of *Henry VI, Part 3* almost overwhelms the playwright. Like a beginner's first sermon, it makes too many points. There are at least eight protagonists who open their hearts to us. The play is a crowded canvas with too much incident, too many atrocities, and it shows its author as an almost naïvely ardent nationalist.

In keeping with the findings in Appendix A, internal evidence in *Henry VI, Part 3* indicates that it was composed before its author 43 set eyes on London. The name "London" occurs sixteen times in the play, but never once with any vivid sense of personal or firsthand acquaintance with the city. It is used only in expressions like "march to London," "fled to London," and "go to London."

By contrast, in *Henry VI, Part 2* there are hints that by the time it was written, its author knew life in London: "In this city will I stay, and live alone as secret as I may" (4.4.47). He mentions a "pissing-conduit" (4.6.3); he has observed London 'prentice riots: "Fear not thy master; fight for credit of the 'prentices" (2.3.71); there are scenes at the Tower, in Cannon Street, in Smithfield, in Southwark.

As is also shown in Appendix A, *The Comedy of Errors* was written at about the same time as *Henry VI, Part 3*, or shortly after. With classical comedy for its model, its author achieved considerable mastery of dramatic technique. Doggerel, repetitive answers, verbal quibbles, plot impossibilities, and also the fact that the dialogue sticks literally to the plot incidents, mark it as very early work. It is good theater, but we never find in it any imprint of Shakespeare's thoughtful mind reflecting upon the state of mankind.

The manuscripts of plays in his saddlebags were warranty for believing he might make his fortune as a playwright in London. But when he first glimpsed the buildings of the City looming in the distance, could he foresee his future fame? He knew that the best phrases he could coin or the finest dramatic scenes he could create, would have an uphill fight against plays by the University graduates with their wealth of learning, scholarship, established reputations, and presumable resentment against a newcomer who had little formal education. Whatever self-confidence our poet on horseback had, he had reason to feel apprehensive that he might be defeated in competition with the most polished playwrights who had studied at Oxford and Cambridge. Could his plays succeed against theirs? If he felt a wave of despair at the necessity of rivaling the University Wits in popularity, hope must have flared again with the realization that the judgment of the University Wits would have nothing to do with his success or failure. No indeed. Success would be won by a playwright to the extent that he pleased the great majority of average men in theater audiences. All Shakespeare's plays testify to his determination that every line he wrote would be

44   for the ears and hearts and minds of the spectators. He held to that

decision, with the result that he was *never for one instant out of touch with his theater audience.* This is not to deny that he would say many things whose full significance many persons did not grasp. Even while he kept the attention of his audience, his imagination made long leaps beyond them. At the same time he refutes those who flatter themselves by thinking that extraordinary perception is a prerequisite to understanding him. He trips up those who look for the recondite in him. He ridicules esoteric pretensions. He derides ostentatious didacticism with "mocking merriment," though with such judiciousness that we can never direct at him the taunt, "Your wit makes wise things foolish."

To anyone arriving for the first time, the City seemed a bedlam: the jostling in the streets, the cries of pedlars, the clomping of hoofs on cobblestones, the rumbling of drays, the darting hither and yon of messengers. The human medley seemed a brew pot of cruelty, with smug faces, contorted mouths, quick jeers, brawls and curses. The ale smell of taverns at every turn, the odor of rotting garbage, the stench of excreta and dung heaps, made a stink too foul to be cured by intermittent whiffs of sweet-scented flowers from the many lovingly tended gardens. Here were frocked preachers and furtive pickpockets, robed and awesome justices and daring cutpurses, unsuspecting honest folk and ingenious coney-catchers, alluring prostitutes and lusting apprentices. Here within all hearts were virtue and vice in conflict, but to the discerning viewer most men appeared uncomprehending of themselves, especially the hawkers and tradesmen with their calculating eyes.

If a poet writing plays could catch the attention of this throng and show men to themselves as they are within themselves, what triumphs he might have! Having come to sell Londoners the products of his pen, Shakespeare must have thought, looking into the eyes of one and then another: Will you, Sir, or you, be willing to buy? What will you give for a comedy? What for a history of a famous king? What for a tale that thrills you with horror? How much for laughter? How much for songs? What price a poet's dreams?

There have been guesses, but no certainty, as to the year in which Shakespeare first went up to London.* One guess—that it

* "In 1590 he was, so far as the scanty evidence shows, unknown; for if he was already in London and already beginning to attract attention to himself, no record

45

was a year sooner than generally accepted—seems to have been
linked with the erroneous assumption that he first turned to writing
plays after he arrived in London. The extra year there allowed time
that would make more credible his seemingly incredible progress as
a playwright. Malone, Halliday, and Baldwin think it possible that
he arrived in London in 1587. But the laws governing apprentice-
ships* make it safer to say he arrived in 1588.

Opportunities for a playwright were limited in London, since
there were only three public playhouses which had been built as
such. Two were outside the City wall in Shoreditch: The Theatre,
over ten years old, and near it, The Curtain. The third was across
the river on the Bankside in Southwark not far from the Bear-
Baiting Gardens. It was Philip Henslowe's new theater called The
Rose.

The Oxford-trained John Lyly had written for the common
stages, but had withdrawn from them completely. He was now
writing refined plays for the Choirboys at St. Paul's who performed
in Blackfriars Priory. Lyly was more concerned with preserving the
minds of his boy actors from contamination than he was with
moving the hearts of Londoners. It was obvious to Shakespeare that
in his own playwriting he would not face any competition from
Lyly. But George Peele, also from Oxford, and Robert Greene, who
boasted the dual distinction of having studied at both Cambridge
and Oxford, were not squeamish like Lyly. Both were popular.
However, neither of them had captivated the audiences at any of
the common stages as had Thomas Kyd, who had no university
training and yet had written a play that was as big a hit as any, his
gory and revengeful *Spanish Tragedy*. And there was the new
dramatist, the Cambridge scholar Christopher Marlowe, with his
spectacular and eloquent *Tamburlaine* being played at The Rose with
Edward Alleyn in the title role.

Marlowe was the best poet among the playwrights with whom
Shakespeare entered into competition. Marlowe was a friend of
Thomas Walsingham, a cousin of Sir Francis Walsingham, who was

---

of it has survived. Yet by September 1592 he was sufficiently well known."[1] Obviously
we are compelled to extrapolate into Shakespeare's London career. If by 1592 he
"already had won a considerable reputation as a dramatist"[2] he must have had
several successful plays on the stage in the course of several preceding years.

46   *   See p. 22.

Secretary to the Queen's Privy Council. The Walsinghams were deeply involved in espionage for the Queen's Government. While a divinity student at Corpus Christi College in Cambridge, Marlowe served as a spy, and he was absent from school for a long period. It was being said openly in the university that not only had he been seen in France, in Rheims, but he had gone there intending to stay with other English youths in exile who were being trained to be missionaries in the Catholic effort to restore England to the Papacy. When Marlowe reappeared in Cambridge, so much prejudice had been awakened against him that he was refused the Master's degree for which he applied. Almost immediately, the Queen's Privy Council notified the Cambridge University authorities that they were making a grave misjudgment, and one most displeasing to Her Majesty. The Council ordered that there be no postponement in giving Marlowe his degree:

> Whereas it was reported that Christopher Marlowe was determined to have gone beyond the seas to Reames and there to remaine Their Lordships thought good to certifie that he had no such intent but that in all his accons he had behaved him selfe orderlie and discreetelie wherebie he had done her majestie good service, and deserved to be rewarded for his faithful dealings: Their Lordships' request was that the rumor thereof should be allaied by all possible meanes, and that he should be furthered in the degree he was to take this next commencement: Because it was not her majesties pleasure that anie one emploied as he had been in matters touching the benefit of his Countrie should be defamed by those that are ignorant in th'affaires he went about.[3]

This sensational focusing of public attention upon a student only twenty-three years of age went to the young man's head like wine. It made Marlowe feel that he was specially privileged and could say with impunity things which men who were not so knowledgeable of secret affairs concerning the State could say only with peril to themselves. It tended to add recklessness to a character that was already naturally impulsive.

All London, of course, heard how Marlowe had been praised by the Privy Council's request in 1587, since it entailed a public answering of the gossip about him in Cambridge. It was obvious that Marlowe had pretended to be a Catholic in order to spy on

3*

Catholics. To young Shakespeare it meant that Marlowe, the spy, would be a most dangerous person with whom to have dealings. Young William was aware of the gossip in his home town and the reasons for suspicion (see Chapter 3) that his own father was a recusant and possibly a Papist, but of course he was without foreknowledge that his father would be publicly listed in 1592 as a recusant. Marlowe's having spied on Catholics could not fail to remind Shakespeare that in 1583 two of his mother's kin—Ardens and Catholics—had been involved in a Papist plot to kill Queen Elizabeth, and had been executed. And he knew that Sir Francis Walsingham, Marlowe's patron, had sent an inquisitor to Stratford to find more victims, but the people there had refused to testify against one another. In January 1588, the Privy Council issued an order to apprehend all "popish" recusants. Marlowe presumably would be looking for any slightest word that could be construed as sympathetic toward such recusants. Shakespeare, with years of practice in caution behind him, must have determined to have nothing to do with Christopher Marlowe, or as little to do with him as possible. He would try to avoid meeting Marlowe. He certainly would never engage in serious conversation with him. Above all he would be particularly watchful as to what words passed his lips in any gathering in which Marlowe was present. Even if the university-trained Marlowe had deigned to meet the Stratford shopkeeper's son as an equal, collaboration with Marlowe in playwriting would have been unthinkable to Shakespeare.

With *Tamburlaine, Part 1,* and soon after it, *Part 2,* Marlowe brought a new music into English poetry. In long speeches like "The thirst of reign and sweetness of a crown" (*Part 1,* Act 2, Scene 7), or "If all the pens that ever poets held" (Act 5, Scene 1), he entranced the ears of Londoners with a verse that resounded with melody. He could string lines together into a passage of swelling oratory, as in Tamburlaine's lament for his dying queen (*Part 2,* Act 2, Scene 4):

> Black is the beauty of the brightest day: . . .
> The cherubims and holy seraphims,
> That sing and play before the King of Kings,
> Use all their voices and their instruments
> To entertain divine Zenocrate;

And, in this sweet and curious harmony,
The god that tunes this music to our souls
Holds out his hand in highest majesty
To entertain divine Zenocrate.

This exuberant and impassioned poetry deeply stirred the emotions. Londoners had never heard anything like it. Here were splendid images which, as Wolfgang Clemen says, "correspond to the titanic nature of Tamburlaine."[4] It was great rhetoric, carrying hearers beyond reality into touch with the stars.

Nevertheless, it was lyricism outracing the harness of drama. It was gorgeous declamation, but it delayed the play. In no particular was the personal situation of Tamburlaine advanced by the speech on Zenocrate. It was Marlowe allowing himself the luxury of escape from stagecraft into unleashed poetry.

To see how differently Shakespeare as a beginner (and indeed always) handled poetry in a play, examine the long speeches in any of his plays. Any one of them will serve, though the longer the speech the more scope for lyrical intrusion, were the poet so minded. Let us note the longest speech in *Henry VI, Part 3* (3.2.124–195). Throughout this speech we see that what Shakespeare called "my art" was not a treatise on how to soar with lyric fervor, but how to blend poetry into drama. He avoided declamation and decorative imagery, and held strictly to dramatic motivation. The contrast with Marlowe is instructive. In the longest speech, Richard, Duke of Gloucester, plans to murder his way to the throne. Throughout the speech he analyzes himself and expresses determination to pursue his villainy:

Ay, Edward will use women honourably.
Would he were wasted, marrow, bones, and all,
That from his loins no hopeful branch may spring,
To cross me from the golden time I look for! ...
Why, I can smile, and murder whiles I smile, ...
I can add colours to the chameleon,
Change shapes with Proteus for advantages,
And set the murderous Machiavel to school.
Can I do this, and cannot get a crown?
Tut, were it farther off, I'll pluck it down.

49

Every line of this speech is dramatic, yet there are numerous phrases which we may call lyrical phrases, that are memorable and often quoted.

For a facile lyricist the temptation in writing a play was to introduce, as Marlowe became famous for doing, long lyrical speeches which are eloquent as lyrical poetry but which retard the action on the stage. In this, Shakespeare refused to follow Marlowe. For a poet who had written *Venus and Adonis*, it would have been within Shakespeare's power at any time after he came to London, and even before, to rhapsodize as Marlowe did. He chose instead to experiment in a different direction. Since his primary purpose was to acquire mastery in the field of drama, and make his fortune as a playwright, which he could not do as a lyric poet, he held his lyricism in check until he learned how to bring it into dialogue without interrupting the drama. This could not be achieved by exuberantly jamming lyrical poetry into a play. Lyricism had to be employed with restraint. Shakespeare's aim was not so spectacular as Marlowe's. It was far more complex. His purpose was to be a successful playwright primarily and a poet secondarily. He would never let the poet in him defeat the dramatist. And so he taught himself how to avoid lyrical padding and how to subordinate poetry to the business at hand by so weaving it into the texture of a speech that the images would be fused together with the dramatic elements and would justify themselves by providing imaginative insight into characters, motives, and conflicting impulses.

Colin Wilson in *Bernard Shaw* says: "The purpose of art could be defined as 'escape from Personality'."[5] Shakespeare obviously clings to his own personality in his nondramatic poems, but almost not at all, at least not obviously, in his plays. Starting as a lyric poet, he understood perfectly what he wanted to become—something which at first he was not—a dramatic poet. This is the key to what he called his "art."

Marlowe's grandiloquent speeches—what Ben Jonson called "furious vociferation"—intensify the emotion of the moment. When Shakespeare wishes to intensify the emotion of a moment, he introduces suspense or a clash of wills.

A widely accepted error has been to represent Shakespeare "as beginning his career by laboriously writing second-hand Marlowese."[6] The findings in Appendix A show that Shakespeare did not begin as an imitator of Marlowe. It is true that *Titus Andronicus* and *Richard III* competed with Marlowe's successes, that *The Merchant of Venice* owed some plot material to *The Jew of Malta* and that *Richard II* owed some to *Edward II*. Shakespeare adopted some of Marlowe's ideas and occasionally took a phrase of Marlowe's which haunted him, and put it through the alembic of his imagination to create something new. But in the writing of *Henry VI, Part 3* and *Part 2* Shakespeare preceded Marlowe in the creation of English chronicle histories.* And in Marlowe's *Edward II* "a number of phrases show that his [Marlowe's] ear had been attentive to performances of Henry VI."[7]

We now know that Marlowe moved away from flexibility and freedom, with fewer open lines and more end-stopping. He made the individual line progressively more dominant. In this respect, Shakespeare traveled in the opposite direction. He was experimenting with blank verse of even more rhythmic flow, with fewer and fewer end-of-line pauses. With Marlowe's "mighty line" (as Jonson called it) becoming increasingly end-stopped, Shakespeare was fortunately influenced by Marlowe very slightly. Many commentators have asserted that he copied from Marlowe a trick of sonorousness achieved by polysyllables as in "To entertain divine Zenocrate." If this is all that is meant by Marlowe's "mighty line" and its influence upon Shakespeare, we may accept it. It was something Shakespeare did infrequently.

Shakespeare may have begun to earn his living in London as a serving man with a theater company. As such he would have been called a "groom." The term had no hostler connotation. It is both erroneous and unfair to say of him: "He began more like a plodder than a poet."[8] A serving man of a theater company ran errands and did odd jobs, but he also acted parts for which he was fitted; and if he could write, as Shakespeare had at once showed he could, he was employed as a playwright. Above all other forms of art, theater work is a composite. Plays did not have runs, for in a repertory system a different play was given on each afternoon and so there were grueling rehearsals. Performances in the public playhouses were in the spring and autumn. In summer the company was on the road. In winter there were rehearsals in the

* Shakespeare may also have written *The Famous Victories* in 1586 or earlier.

51

inns in the City, in preparation for a few Court performances and the spring season.

About seven years after writing *Venus and Adonis,* when Shakespeare dedicated it to the Earl of Southampton, he scrupulously made clear that it was early work—"the first heir of my invention"—and that the Earl would be "godfather" at its baptism in print. But because he had not written that poem for the Earl, he vowed to "take advantage of all idle hours" till he had honored the Earl "with some graver labour." Perhaps the poet had become critical of his early work, almost apologetic.

We do not know Shakespeare's writing habits, what time of day he did his best work, the rate of his ingestion of source material, or his speed of composition. We do know what is far more important—the concepts which guided him as a beginner. We are made aware of them through the works which we now recognize as having been written during his pre-London years. And we note two books which gave advice to would-be authors during those years.

Thomas Wilson in *Arte of Rhetorique,* opposed frequent quotations from Latin. Shakespeare would have welcomed Wilson's disapproval of archaisms and words not in everyday use, and his counsel against "inkhorn terms"—affectations borrowed from foreign languages. It was easy for Shakespeare to welcome Wilson's advice against a parade of learning because he himself had less book learning to parade than most poets of his day, but he also knew that a parade of learning was a block against audience enjoyment.

George Gascoigne's *Certayne Notes of Instruction in English Verse* (1575) gave still more lively and provocative advice. Shakespeare may have given some heed to Gascoigne's counsel as to the length of words a poet should use. Gascoigne said:

> I thinke it not amisse to forewarne you that you thrust as few wordes of many syllables into your verse as may be; and hereunto I might alledge many reasons: first the most auncient English wordes are of one syllable, so that the more monosyllables that you use, the truer Englishman you shall seeme. . . . Wordes of one syllable will more easily fall to be short or long as occasion requireth, or wilbe adapted to become circumflexe or of an indifferent sounde. . . . I do not meane hereby that you may use none other wordes but of twoo sillables, for therein you may use discretion according to occasion of matter.

52

Gascoigne's counsel against polysyllables was in line with his further advice: "As much as you may, frame your stile to perspicacity and to be sensible; for the haughty obscure verse doth not much delight."

A constant feature of Shakespeare's style is that he never resorts to deliberate complexities, as though "the end of study" were "things hid and barr'd from common sense." He describes himself as a man of "true plain words" (Sonnet 82) who defends and exalts "simple truth miscall'd simplicity" (Sonnet 86). The two lines quoted below are in a description Troilus gives of himself, but their substance is applicable to Shakespeare:

> Whiles others fish with craft for great opinion,
> I with great truth catch mere simplicity.
> [*Troilus and Cressida*, 4.4.103–104]

Lest this emphasis be misinterpreted, we note that while Shakespeare's vocabulary and style are simple, he does not give a simple answer to life's problems. He shows unresolvable opposites, and thus reflects the mystery of life. This duality keeps his plays "out of the reach of the narrow moralist, the special pleader for a particular ideology. . . . It is that mode of vision that puts the plays beyond philosophy and makes them works of art."[9]

Endowed with intellectual energy, and with unfaltering determination to succeed, Shakespeare wrote plays in spare hours, with faith that they would "prove a good repast to the spectators."[10] The first plays he sold in London were bought from him with all rights thereto, and the top price for a play was £6.13.4, equivalent in modern purchasing power to about $750. His plays became the property of the acting company, and since his name was unknown to the public, they were at first anonymous. Publication of a play was something an acting company tried to prevent, for there was no copyright and a rival company would certainly present a play if they could get hold of its text. Publicity for Shakespeare was thus for some years by word of mouth on the part of spectators and his fellow players. Not until 1598 did his name appear on the title page of a printed play. He benefited from his plays at the beginning only indirectly through the added prosperity their popularity brought to the company.

Individualism was unrestrained and rampant in the reign of Queen Elizabeth. An Englishman was permitted to do what he wanted to do so long as he did not cause the authorities to feel their power was being endangered. If he injured others, that was their hard luck. Costly lawsuit was the only protection one man had against another. Writers who could not afford legal redress were particularly vulnerable, and were often victimized. While the public derided plagiarism of even so little as a single line, there was no law making it illegal to steal whole plays in pirated editions. A playwright's stock-in-trade was what he created with his brain, but businessmen, called "adventurers," could take all the profits from what the playwright had written if they could get hold of the text. It was a golden age of individualism.

While Shakespeare was beginning to shape his career in London, a book was published there in 1589 which probably influenced his writing. This was Puttenham's *The Arte of English Poesie*. When Puttenham asked "Why should not Poesie be a vulgar art?" he was not giving approval to all that the word vulgar now includes, such as offenses against refined taste, but he was embracing far more than the university scholars were willing to do. By "vulgar" he meant the vernacular; not Latin or Greek, but English. He was also proposing a revolutionary step, for he advocated the poet's use of the nonliterary English of "the meaner sort of men," and to explain "meaner" he specified "serving men, yeomen, grooms."

Puttenham was for poetry as against prose: "Utterance in prose is not of so great efficacie because dayly used and by that occasion the eare is overglutted with it, but is also not so voluble and slipper upon the tong." While Shakespeare was no doubt impressed with this argument, he saw dramatic situations in which prose seemed preferable to verse, especially in comedies and where he felt humor was needed in chronicle histories and even in tragedies. Twenty-five percent of Shakespeare's plays are in prose.

In respect to subject matter admissible in poetry, Puttenham allowed the "vaine, dissolute, or wanton, so it be not very scandalous and of evill example." Without lessening of moral earnestness, Shakespeare expressed the "vaine, dissolute, or wanton" with frolicsome naturalness. His bawdry flouted the straitlaced morality of the Puritans. Some of his sex jokes might have caused even

54

Puttenham to blush. Lindley Murray in the eighteenth century bewailed this and said Shakespeare caused "fatal wounds to youth's innocence, delicacy, and religion." Let us say rather that Shakespeare rescued youth from naïveté, fastidiousness, and sectarianism. Arland Usher in his introduction to *The Ginger Man* says: "The right cure for dirty-mindedness is the cultivation of the comic sense." Shakespeare's bridge to the minds of many in his audience was rakehellish wit. The actual effect, however, was to insulate against evil by ribs of laughter.

Shakespeare never attempted to be preacher or philosopher, but was content as poet dramatist to write actable scenes. He knew supremely well what was speakable. He did not let any desire to be "literary" run away with him. He avoided "strained touches rhetoric can lend."[11]

His contacts with university-trained men during his first year in London brought a sharp increase in syllabic intensity. While he indulged in excessive wordplay and punning, a practice he never relinquished,* he was amazingly free of pretentiousness. He never fell into slavish imitation of the mannerisms or stylistic curbs of any of the University Wits.

Audience reactions assured Shakespeare that he had a distinctive style. He wisely did not attempt to change this style to make it resemble that of any of his competitors. He held to it, and let it develop naturally. He recognized it as his own (Sonnet 76), and we recognize it as the stamp of his personality. He could be himself and, as he soon discovered and proved to everyone, in being himself, he could more than compete with the University Wits.

Under compulsion ever since he came to London to prove himself in competition with those who looked upon him as having too little learning, Shakespeare more than met the challenge in 1594–95. He won almost all hearts by "the elegancy, facility and golden cadence" of supremely great poetry which he showed could be made to serve dramatic purposes in a tragedy, a chronicle history, and a comedy—*Romeo and Juliet, Richard II*, and *Midsummer Night's Dream*.

* M. M. Mahood in *Shakespeare's Wordplay* tells us there are more than three thousand instances of wordplay, punning, or near punning in Shakespeare's works, an average of seventy-eight per play.

Richard David has said that "*Romeo* is the last and greatest of Shakespeare's dramatic works, by which I mean those plays in which the dramatic action is . . . ordered (or disordered) by the methods of non-dramatic poetry."[12]

It is fair to ask what David means by "methods of non-dramatic poetry" in *Romeo and Juliet*. Whether we call poetry in a play dramatic or nondramatic surely depends upon the way it is used. Can anyone call Romeo's ecstasy at first sight of Juliet "non-dramatic"? That poetry is part of the throbbing moment: "O! she doth teach the torches to burn bright." This lyrical outpouring does not make the moment less dramatic. Nor can the poetry whispered in the orchard balcony scene be called nondramatic. *Romeo and Juliet* is impassioned drama filled with lyric poetry which is at the same time dramatic since it never merely decorates but always serves the emotions of those who "burn in love."

The story of the lovers in Verona was a prescription for lyric poetry. Having kept an absolute curb upon such poetry in previous playwriting, while using sonnets as an escape valve, Shakespeare in *Romeo and Juliet* unleashed what had long been under strict control.

The dramatic handling of lyric poetry in *Romeo and Juliet* demonstrates the mastery toward which Shakespeare had been striving from the beginning of his career. The quality of poetry in *Richard II* also shows how he had taught himself to incorporate lyricism into the fabric of drama. His gradual attainment of this purpose is evidence that he had known his own lyric power before coming to London, as the author of *Venus and Adonis* could not have failed to know it.

His conscious problem had been how to make himself the supreme poetic dramatist. He had not curbed his poetic imagination but had rigorously steered it to serve his ambition as playwright. In *Midsummer Night's Dream*, at the beginning of Act 5, he found opportunity, without surrendering his purpose, to give Theseus, Duke of Athens, lines as marvelous as poet ever penned. Hippolyta remarks to her husband:

'Tis strange, my Theseus, that these lovers speak of.

Theseus replies:

More strange than true: I never may believe
These antique fables, nor these fairy toys.
Lovers and madmen have such seething brains,
Such shaping fantasies, that apprehend
More than cool reason ever comprehends.
The lunatic, the lover, and the poet
Are of imagination all compact:
One sees more devils than vast hell can hold,
That is, the madman: the lover, all as frantic,
Sees Helen's beauty in a brow of Egypt:
The poet's eye, in a fine frenzy rolling,
Doth glance from heaven to earth, from earth to heaven;
And as imagination bodies forth
The forms of things unknown, the poet's pen
Turns them to shapes, and gives to airy nothing
A local habitation and a name.
Such tricks hath strong imagination.

This famous and lengthy reply by Theseus describes disembodied flights, but is itself in no sense a disembodied flight, or
disconnected lyric outpouring. It is an essential contribution to
the dramatic business of *Midsummer Night's Dream*, and is threaded
into the conversation.

Some of the scholar playwrights had thought Shakespeare's
simple truth was mere simplicity. With subtle purpose he staged
a gentle satire on the Gentlemen Scholars in the reception Duke
Theseus gave to the players—"hard-handed men that work . . .
which never labour'd in their minds till now." It would not serve
his purpose to have Duke Theseus and his courtiers find cause
only for laughter in the absurd mistakes made by the "crew of
patches, rude mechanicals" as they misdeliver the lines of their
"merry and tragical" play. And so when the Master of the Revels
tells Theseus the play is "extremely stretch'd and conn'd with
cruel pain," Theseus says:

> never any thing can be amiss,
> When simpleness and duty tender it. . . .
> Our sport shall be to take what they mistake:
> And what poor duty cannot do, noble respect
> Takes it in might, not merit. . . .
> Love . . . and tongue-tied simplicity
> In least speak most   [5.1. 82–83, 90–92, 104–105]

57

This "noble respect" was a lesson in courtesy to some of those who had opposed Shakespeare, as was also the conversation between Theseus and Hippolyta:

HIPPOLYTA   This is the silliest stuff that ever I heard.
THESEUS   The best in this kind are but shadows; and the worst are no worse, if imagination amend them.
HIPPOLYTA   It must be your imagination then, and not theirs.
THESEUS   If we imagine no worse of them than they of themselves, they may pass for excellent men

[5.1.212–216]

It was essential to Shakespeare's purpose to show that Theseus was capable of being as snobbish as any intellectual, and so he gave him a line as sarcastic as any by a Broadway first nighter:

THESEUS   This passion, and the death of a dear friend, would go near to make a man look sad

[5.1.279–280]

Smothering his private reactions, however, Theseus acts a true gentleman. He publicly pleases the players by pronouncing their play "a fine tragedy . . . very notably discharged."

The magic most to be admired in *Midsummer Night's Dream* is not Oberon's or Titania's or Puck's. It is the way Shakespeare catches in the net of his understanding the snobbishness of cultured persons who enjoy being sarcastic toward the linguistic limitations of men with much less formal education than themselves. It is the way he transforms their pettiness into the breadth of sympathy that makes Duke Theseus use the words "excellent men." Shakespeare had not been soured by the sneers of envious playwrights. He triumphed over them in Act 5 of *Midsummer Night's Dream* with a sweetness that put haughty insolence to shame.

8

MORE THAN
DRUNKEN

" Now, while the world is bent my deeds to cross,"

SONNET 90

*T*HE UNIVERSITY SCHOLARS IN ELIZABETHAN TIMES
conceived of Poetry (which they always spelled with a
capital P) as a divinely inspired but also schooled talent to be used
for the pleasuring and edification of those who had enough
learning to appreciate it. They considered the very soul of Poetry to
be conceits of a cultured flavor. To them, truly great conceits were
scintillating jewels of literary art, requiring a classical air, a courtly
grace, a cloistered rarity, a loftiness out of touch with anything
common. To use Nash's impudent phrase in 1589, such conceits
could not be achieved by a "home-borne mediocritie." Poetry was a
tool of snobbishness.

Shakespeare, in self-defense a year or two later, was satirical
of the kind of poetry the university scholars admired:

59

What, my soul, verses?

Ay, sir, and very learned.

[*Love's Labour's Lost*, 4.2.105–106]

Shakespeare knew that his own style was simple and unique, but he also knew that style alone would not win success. He had to find provocative subject matter. He observed the appetite for cruelty in men and women, and their large capacity for righteous indignation against bestial behavior in persons they could condemn without besmirching themselves. He knew that most people would welcome a play in which atrocious cruelty is sentimentally larded with appeal to pity. He would give them such a drama, a tragedy that would satisfy the most passionate thirst for gore.

Titus Andronicus has been called "that odious play . . . a pandemonium of brutality and nightmare horrors."[1] Soft-skinned bardolators have wished that Shakespeare had not written it. Some have eased their thoughts by denying that he did write it. As for his authorship, what more is needed than that it was named as his by Francis Meres in 1598, and that it was included in the First Folio? Hereward T. Price writes perceptively: "No other playwright of that period could carry such a crowd of persons in his brain and make them so different from one another and so alive. . . . No other dramatist could conceive or depict so intense a conflict of characters."[2]

Titus was more than a bid for popularity. However regrettable it has seemed to some, the writing of it was a necessity. "How could a developing genius among humankind do otherwise, if he was to grow? It was Shakespeare's rooting deeply in black soil in order later to flourish like a green bay tree."[3]

Here was the lusty author of *Titus*, a phenomenal new force in the theater, drawing audiences away from bull-baiting and bear-baiting.* To accomplish this feat, he had villains cut off a girl's tongue and hands so that neither by speech nor in writing could she name those who had done her more shameful damage. These appalling amputations were as thoroughly human as the blood-spouting in the Smithfield executions enjoyed by many Londoners, in which, after the condemned had been hanged inconclusively,

---

* In 1591 there was "a royal edict forbidding stage plays on certain days (Sundays and Thursdays) lest they interfere with the audiences at these sports."[5]

his belly was ripped open and his entrails drawn out and burned before his eyes, and in a spectacular climax for the pleasuring of the beholders, his limbs pulled off in the quartering. To become the author of the tragedies we most admire, Shakespeare had to write *Titus*. We can only surmise whether, at the time he wrote it, he had in imagination any of the great tingling masterpieces ahead. M. C. Bradbrook says: "In the laments of Titus which are the core of the piece, can be felt some faint foreshadowing of the pain and madness that were ultimately to issue in *King Lear*."[4]

There was another and presumably earlier play, *Titus and Vespasia*, which has not survived, to which some have supposed *Titus Andronicus* was indebted. Nothing in *Titus Andronicus*, however, points to the Roman Emperor Titus, son of Vespasian.

When was *Titus Andronicus* written?* E. B. Everitt dates it 1588–89. Shakespeare's contemporary Ben Jonson, who prided himself on scholarly carefulness, wrote in 1614 in his introduction to *Bartholomew Fair*: "He that will swear, *Jeronimo*† or *Andronicus* are the best plays yet, shall pass unexpected at here, as a man whose judgment shows it to be constant, and hath stood still these five-and-twenty years."

Five-and-twenty years previous to 1614 is 1589. But Ben Jonson's "five-and-twenty" may not have been precise testimony and may have been merely a way of indicating an approximate quarter of a century. However, since the findings in Appendix A point to 1589 and there are further evidences, the statement of Ben Jonson cannot be summarily dismissed.

Let us have a close look at Thomas Nash's "Prefix" to Robert Greene's *Menaphon*, which was entered for publication on August 23, 1589. Some have held that the "Prefix" attacked only Thomas Kyd. Some have thought it was aimed at Marlowe. Some have thought it was also aimed at Shakespeare, and some that it was aimed exclusively at Shakespeare.

---

* "Sussex's Men who had spent a decade as a provincial organization . . . were back in London in January 1592. . . . Their repertoire consisted of old plays, *Titus Andronicus* being the only one which Henslowe marked as new."[6] *Titus Andronicus* could have been new by comparison with the others in the repertoire at any time during the second half of the decade.

† *Jeronimo* (Hieronimo in Thomas Kyd's *The Spanish Tragedy*) mentioned first by Jonson, is generally believed to have been an earlier play, about 1587.

61

Nash's phrasing in the "Prefix" is in the plural, and at first glance does not seem to refer to a single poet. But Richard Simpson strongly argues that the third sentence of it, in spite of its use of the plural, does refer to a single poet.[7]

Here is a passage from *Titus Andronicus* and one from Nash's "Prefix":

> . . . notwithstanding all this loss of blood,
> As from a conduit with three issuing spouts,
> Yet do thy cheeks look red as Titan's face
> Blushing to be encounter'd with a cloud.
>
> [*Titus*, 2.4.29–32]

> servile imitation of vainglorious tragoedians, who contend not so seriouslie to excell in action, as to embowell the cloudes in a speach of comparison.
>
> [Nash]

We now face three possibilities: that *Titus Andronicus* and Nash's "Prefix" had no bearing upon each other; that Nash had witnessed a performance of *Titus Andronicus* and in his "Prefix" was condemning the nonsense in it. (See the rest of the long speech by Marcus [47 lines], from which the four lines above have been quoted); that Shakespeare was so crassly insensitive that after the publication of the "Prefix" he deliberately wrote into *Titus Andronicus* extravagances which would glaringly illustrate what Nash had intelligently ridiculed.

Here are other passages:

> my bowels cannot hide her woes,
> But like a drunkard I must vomit them.
> Then give me leave; for losers will have leave
> To ease their stomachs with their bitter tongues.
>
> [*Titus*, 3.1.231–234]

> oercloieth their imagination with a more than drunken resolution, beeing not extemporal in the invention of anie other meanes to vent their manhood, commits the digestion of their choleric incumbrances, to the spacious volubilities of a drumming decasillabon.
>
> [Nash]

And again two passages:

> repose you here in rest,
> Secure from worldly chances and mishaps!
> Here lurks no treason, here no envy swells,
> Here grow no damned grudges; here are no storms,
> No noise, but silence and eternal sleep.
>
> [*Titus*, 1.1.152–155]

mongst this kinde of men that repose eternitie in the mouth of a player.

[Nash]

Which of the three possibilities do we accept? How about the castigations in the next passages?:

CHIRON   O, 'tis a verse in Horace; I know it well: I read it in the grammar long ago.

AARON   Ay, just; a verse in Horace; right, you have it.
[*Aside*] Now, what a thing it is to be an ass!

[*Titus*, 4.2.22–25]

I can but ingrosse some deepe read Grammarians, who having no more learning in their brain, than will serve to take up a commoditie; nor Arte in their brain, than was nourished in a serving man's idelnesse, will take upon them to be the ironical censors of all, when God and Poetrie doth know, they are the simplest of all.

[Nash]

What shall we say: No applicability whatsoever? Nash sneering at an author who quotes Latin familiar to every schoolboy and thereby flaunts his insufficiency? The poet parading his own academic limitations in wilful contempt of scholarly censure?

Here are two more passages, the first spoken by Aaron:

> Now climbeth Tamora Olympus' top,
> Safe out of fortune's shot; and sits aloft,
> Secure of thunder's crack or lightning's flash, . . .
> Then, Aaron, arm thy heart, and fit thy thoughts,
> To mount aloft with thy imperial mistress,

63

And mount her pitch, whom thou in triumph long
Hast prisoner held, fetter'd in amorous chains,
And faster bound to Aaron's charming eyes
Than is Prometheus tied to Caucasus.

[*Titus*, 2.1.1–3, 12–17]

alcumists of eloquence, who (mounted on the stage of arrogance)
think to outbrave better pens with the swelling bumbast of a bragging
blanke verse.

[Nash]

What is the final verdict of the jury? The safest conclusion
seems to be that Nash had witnessed a performance of *Titus
Andronicus* which had moved him to express in his "Prefix" in 1589
his condemnation of what he felt to be its absurdities.

Meticulous search through Kyd's *The Spanish Tragedy* and both
parts of Marlowe's *Tamburlaine* has found no passages to which the
five statements quoted from Nash's "Prefix" can by any stretch of
the imagination be said to apply. In *The Spanish Tragedy*, the word
"mount" is used once in each of two scenes, 3.7.11–14 and 3.8.15,
without conceivable imputation of arrogance.

They do appear persuasively to apply to *Titus Andronicus*. They,
along with the corroborating evidence of Ben Jonson's dating, and
the dating in Appendix A, seem to establish beyond any question
that *Titus Andronicus* was on the boards in 1589.

9

GROWTH IN EARLY PLAYS

"To give full growth to that which still doth grow."

SONNET 115

*T*HE REMARKABLE BALANCE OF SHAKESPEARE'S temperament is seen in the fact that within a few months of the time that he wrote the horrifying *Titus Andronicus,* he penned a sprightly comedy. He seems to have borrowed plot material for it from the same source used by the author of a rival comedy, although he may have borrowed directly from the rival play. Some prefer to think the author of the rival play borrowed from Shakespeare. The anonymous author and Shakespeare both make use of a drunken sot, Christopher Sly, before whom the play itself is performed, and the two comedies are parallel in subject matter. The rival comedy is believed to have reached the boards first. It had an excellent title, *The Taming of a Shrew.* It was popular enough to be published in 1594, and reprinted in 1596 and again in 1607.

Shakespeare's comedy had to establish itself as a new play, different from its competitor. To do that it perforce had to bear a very different title.* For at least the first twenty years of its existence, it could not be called by the almost identical title, *The Taming of the Shrew*. There was no legal objection, but it would obviously have been a borrowed title, which would have undesirably advertised the parallelism in plot, and would have caused confusion. We have evidence that Shakespeare's comedy was given a makeshift title, *Loves labours wonne*. That evidence is this: Francis Meres in *Palladis Tamia*, entered in 1598, sought to show that Shakespeare deserved to rank with the greatest dramatists of ancient times. To do this Meres named those plays which in his opinion justified his assertion. He mentioned, by naming the kings, all the chronicle histories of Shakespeare up to that time, with the exception of *Henry VI*, which many would agree he showed good judgment in omitting from a list given to "witness" to the supreme greatness of Shakespeare. Meres also mentioned all the tragedies of Shakespeare up to that time. The presumption is therefore strong that his separate list of comedies included all Shakespeare's comedies up to that time. One of the comedies he mentioned was *Loves labours wonne*. There is no reason to doubt that this was the comedy whose title was later changed to *The Taming of the Shrew*, because if this is not what happened, then we are compelled to accept two assumptions, each of them incredible: that Shakespeare's *Loves labours wonne* was completely forgotten by fellow members of his acting company when they were preparing the First Folio; and that Meres forgot to mention a comedy of so popular a nature as *The Taming of the Shrew*, which Appendix A shows to have been written— and which most scholars agree was written—several years previous to the statement by Meres.

Loves labours wonne was an unsatisfactory title because it was too revealingly descriptive. There was no promise of suspense in a title which told an audience that the lovers would overcome all opposition to their union. It spoiled the surprise in the all-important final scene, in which Katerina's speech pays tribute to the "painful labour" by which a loving husband maintains his wife. It shows us that what has been "wonne" is not merely the enjoyment

* Nothing in the text of a play is so acutely conformable to audience reactions as is its title, the feature to which box-office receipts are most sensitive.

of love's pleasures, but the recognition of the responsibilities of marriage.

Shakespeare's was by far the better play. In the course of time it became more popular than *The Taming of a Shrew*. Eventually, when that rival comedy had been well forgotten by the public—that is, several years after the 1607 edition of *The Taming of a Shrew*, or about the time the First Folio was published in 1623—the desirable title *The Taming of the Shrew* became admissible for Shakespeare's play. That title was first used, so far as we have record, in the First Folio.

Shakespeare's next comedy had a contrasting and alliterative and far superior title, *Love's Labour's Lost*. This comedy was written by a playwright who was not yet a master craftsman, who was still in the workshop. The play was bogged down with two hundred puns. While this comedy was "new corrected and augmented" to be acted before the Queen at Christmas 1598, and again revised for Christmas 1604, there is no reason to suppose that the text as we have it is not essentially the same in theme, characters, and action as when it was first produced. Allusions were no doubt retouched and brought up to date in the two revisions, and new bits added, but the original conception and the features that made the play popular were certainly not discarded.

Written in the period when Shakespeare was composing the bulk of his sonnets, *Love's Labour's Lost* introduces various forms, but it also has much prose. Indeed, one-third of the play is prose, and it gives a foretaste of ten later plays which have a larger percentage, six of them with more than half prose.

Love's Labour's Lost ridicules men who promise each other they will never love a woman. It also ridicules the schoolmaster Holofernes, and the fantastical Spaniard, Don Adriano de Armado. The satire of the men who swear they will never fall in love with a woman, because they do not want their studies to be interrupted, is Shakespeare's psychological compensation for not having studied at a university like most of his competitors. He disapproved of any man who would "blunt his natural edge with . . . study."[1] With youthful zest he unmercifully satirized the scholar Holofernes. Keen thinks that the character of this dull pedant may have been conceived from William Stanley's tutor, the pompous pedagogue Richard Floyd, at New Park in Lancashire.

67

The name Armado is an allusion to the Spanish Armada. Elizabethan audiences held Don Armado in derision. He is a caricature of a Spanish gallant, with the polished elegance of a gentleman, but a braggard:

> One whom the music of his own vain tongue
> Doth ravish like enchanting harmony.
> [*Love's Labour's Lost*, 1.1.166–167]

Was Shakespeare slanting at Marlowe?

The character of Armado was the first in any of Shakespeare's plays to make a hit on the London stage. Internal evidence in the play takes kindly to the idea that Shakespeare acted the part. Armado ends Act I: "Assist me some extemporal god of rhyme, for I am sure I shall turn sonnet. Devise, wit; write, pen; for I am for whole volumes in folio." At the end of Act 5 Armado steps forward as the spokesman for the entire company, an indication that, if its author was an actor in the play, this was the part he took.*

Shakespeare's first four comedies, in the order in which we now know they were written, show consistent growth in the quality of humor, from mere humor of situation to humor of characterization.

Shakespeare's first four chronicle histories, in the order in which we now know they were written, similarly show consistent growth. In his first, *Henry VI, Part 3*, the historical material overburdens the dramatist. *Henry VI, Part 2* is less contentious and far more interesting. The chief criticism would be that the various incidents are not brought into unity. In his third chronicle history, *Richard III*, he warps history, revamps it for his own purposes, and falsifies it factually, but he is so thoroughly in command of his medium that he creates a psychologically true and complex character in his hero-villain, and thus gives the play a unity which his first two chronicle histories lack

In his fourth chronicle history, *Henry VI, Part 1*, he starts with the action of a war, told with thrilling suspense. The hero Talbot

---

* In his painting (1604) of Shakespeare and Ben Jonson playing chess, Karel van Mander (†1606) pictures Shakespeare with Spanish collar and sombrero type hat, presumably his stage costume as Don Armado. Scratched on the back of the picture's original oak frame was "W. S.—Armado."

dominates from the first scene to the end of Act 4, achieving the almost impossible: "Valiant Talbot above human thought enacted wonders." With patriotic fervor, the play invokes vibrant words: "English Henry," and "God and Saint George, Talbot and England's right." To enhance patriotic emotion, Shakespeare resorts to extravagance and heroics. The Talbot scenes of Act 4 are in rhyme, which, briefly done, has the emotional effect of song. Talbot pleads with his son to save his own life. The son matches his father in courageous pose: "If I fly, I am not Talbot's son." Old Talbot is mortally wounded; his dead son is borne in; Talbot grieves as he dies. After the death of Talbot, is anything left for England? Yes, of course. Act 5 shows what.

Henry VI, Part 1 shares obloquy with *Titus* as a play in which some of the subject matter has aroused intense dislike, which in turn has colored many judgments as to the quality of its poetry. There has been resentment at Shakespeare's characterization of Joan, his making her—at the climax of her self-defense—admit dishonesty, and claim to be with child, naming several men. Instead of leaving the stage as a virgin with the respect of the audience, she leaves it as a liar and a whore.

To what extent do the Joan la Pucelle scenes actually violate history? They certainly violate modern sentiment. However, in Elizabethan times as in the early fifteenth century, the English believed Joan of Arc to be a witch with "familiars" who were fiends. Shakespeare pictures her as a maid up to her final scene. Perhaps in that scene the guards twist her arms, and she screams in agony, and thus her plea for stay of execution because of pregnancy is wrung from her. It could be that Shakespeare intended the scene to be acted so that thoughtful beholders would understand that Joan's confessions are forced and false.

Shakespeare's progress in ability to weave poetry into dialogue not with rhapsodizing flights but with lyrically expressed dramatic details that never clog the action may be seen in the opening speeches of his first four chronicle histories, for those speeches are a fair sampling of each play. The first two speeches of *Henry VI, Part 3* are plain statement of fact without poetic dressing. The first speech of *Henry VI, Part 2* is more personalized, though scarcely more poetic. In Gloucester's speech, which is the beginning of *Richard III*, imagery heightens the characterization, and there is constant   69 use of poetic figures, but every phrase contributes to the narrative element. In the first two speeches of *Henry VI, Part 1* there is a distinct advance in poetic fervor, an unleashing of lyricism with emotional vigor, yet imagery is held attuned to the dramatic purpose.

Shakespeare's fourth chronicle history brought him the first critical acclaim he received from any of the scholars. "If *1 Henry VI* was written for Strange's Men in the new theatre (The Rose) it must have been composed before 1591/2."[2] In *Pierce Penilesse his Supplication to the Divell,* 1592, Nash gives a sociological argument for the common stages, and in it he commends the part of Talbot in *Henry VI, Part 1.* Nash had been caught by the blatant appeal to patriotism. His reference to "Talbot" was unquestionably to the Talbot in *Henry VI, Part 1,* at least in absence of a Talbot in any other surviving play.

> How would it have joyed brave Talbot (the terror of the French) to thinke that after he had layn two hundred years in his Toomb, he should triumph againe on the Stage, and have his bones new embalmed with the teares of 10 thousand spectators at least (at severall times) who, in the Tragedies* that represent his person, imagine they behold him fresh bleeding.

Nash mentions the students of the Inns of Court as forming part of the London theater audiences. Far more than any other Englishmen, students of law were trained to appreciate the various meanings and implications of words. The presence of many law students in his audiences was an inducement to Shakespeare to make frequent use of legal terms in his plays. With wit and industry and with boyhood memories of legal phrases he had heard from the lips of his father,† he provided entertainment for exacting and discriminating men of law.

---

* The "Tragedies" were Talbot's being hopelessly overpowered because of the Duke of Somerset's delay in sending reinforcements, Talbot's defeat by the sorceries of a witch, his inability to persuade his son to save his life by flight, his being mortally wounded, the death of his son, his own death.

† John Shakespeare as High Bailiff of Stratford was Justice of the Peace and Judge of the Court of Record.

70

10

ALL FRAILTIES

*"In my nature reign'd
All frailties that besiege all kinds of blood."*

SONNET 109

W E SEE IN APPENDIX B THAT MOST OF THE DARK
Lady sonnets were written before Shakespeare began
writing sonnets to his friend. The experiences which initiated these
poems stand clear against the background of time, and the time
helps point to the place. Our new knowledge requires a new look
at all the sonnets.

Through the years distance separated our poet from his wife
for periods of many months. There is every reason to believe that she
remained in Stratford with her children while he was on the road or
serving in some manor house. Similarly, when he went to London,
he continued to be separated from his wife for long periods of time.
He was among strangers at first, and felt the losses and gains in
his anonimity in the city. By 1588 he was writing sonnets about his
mistress, whose residence patently was accessible from his own, and

therefore almost certainly was in London. *The Dark Lady filled a need, but she did not assuage his loneliness.

The ancients conceived of Cupid as blind. As to what a votary of love fails to see, no one has ever told us with such clear vision as Shakespeare in his sonnets. He was able to do this because he saw his own blindness.

The quality most constantly discernible in Shakespeare is a clash of opposites. In most of his writings he deals with incompatibilities of character in unresolved and unresolvable conflict, with confused situations that vibrate with the reality of life itself. He does this in *Hamlet,* in *Troilus and Cressida,* and in many other plays. He does it in the contrast between *Venus and Adonis,* where sexual insecurity causes a male to shrink from a female, and in *The Rape of Lucrece,* where lust causes a male to force possession of a female.

In the Dark Lady sonnets, 127 to 152, Shakespeare tells what incompatibilities he finds within himself. The internal conflict is most movingly stated.

Commending the sonnet form to aspirants to fame, George Gascoigne said:

> If I should disclose my pretense in love, I would either make a strange discourse of some intollerable passion, ... or use the covertest means that I could to avoyde the uncomelye customes of common writers.

In Sonnets 127 to 152 Shakespeare explicitly confesses an illicit love. He sees ravishing beauty in a lady who has black eyes and hair (Sonnets 130, 132). This was in defiance of the Petrarchian fashion for blondes. Brunettes, at least in poets' eyes, had suffered such disadvantages that they resorted to hair dyes—"fairing the foul with art's false borrow'd face" (Sonnet 127).

In violation of his marriage vow, Shakespeare made the Dark Lady his mistress. His infatuation with her was an intolerable passion. Sonnet 128, as vivid as a Vermeer, pictures the Dark Lady playing at the virginals, tickling the jacks. The sexual significance is

* The theory that Mary Fitton was his mistress is untenable, for she was born in 1578. Therefore when Shakespeare wrote the sonnets to the Dark Lady, Mary was only ten years old.

72

intensified by a double play of meaning. As much as any of Shakespeare's sonnets, this one communicates the reality of the moment. It creates an impression of aliveness not exceeded by his description of Cleopatra on her barge. Here in Sonnet 128 is the appeal of sex in preliminary play, rousing lust for possession.

In the very next sonnet, the poet excoriates what he has just pictured as irresistibly alluring:

> The expense of spirit in a waste of shame
> Is lust in action; . . .
> Enjoy'd no sooner than despised straight,
> Past reason hunted, and no sooner had
> Past reason hated, . . .
> All this the world well knows; yet none knows well
> To shun the heaven that leads men to this hell.
>
> [Sonnet 129]

Nowhere else in the world's literature is the conflict between body and spirit drawn in sharper contrast than in Sonnets 128 and 129. The poet's predicament reflects the training he had received from religious parents. By his character and breeding, stemming from respect for his father and his mother, he was compelled to combat fleshly impulses. Inevitably, he became a battleground.

His passion for his mistress should not obscure the opposing fact to which the Dark Lady sonnets are eloquent testimony—that Shakespeare had a spiritual nature as strongly developed as in any poet who ever wrote. Without attempting to define "spiritual," let us say he had thirst for self-mastery, joy in creativity, and yearning for ecstatic soaring of heart and mind as potent as the demands of sex. Physical sex was for him a defeat of spirit.

He was so mature in most ways we need not shrink from noting that, as described in the sonnets, he did not enter into creative relationship with the opposite sex. In Sonnets 141 and 142 he calls the intolerable passion for the Dark Lady "sin." His use of "sin" in the sex connotation was in the vocabulary of his day. Sin was feeling an emotion, entertaining a thought, or performing an act contrary to religious proscription. Between his time and our own, religious fanatics have gone to such ridiculous extremes that for intellectuals "morality" is a dirty word, and the word "sin" taboo.

73

At the turn of this century, preachers condemned the new horseless carriages as instruments of sin on two unanswerable counts: people would travel in them for pleasure on Sunday, and a young couple might take a drive in an automobile without a chaperone. Shakespeare was no such fool. He wrote to raise laughs; he acted in the theater; he often traveled on Sundays; and his meetings with the Dark Lady were without chaperone, but only these meetings were "sin."

There is no indication that Shakespeare's struggle against what he called "sin" was an attempt to placate an offended deity. The clear implications are that he sought to build tension by postponement of sex, like electrical voltage, for a channeling of energies which he would devote to his Art. Yet he could not make himself a eunuch. Nowadays we are told it is more "healthy" to satisfy sexual impulses than to resist them. For those who accept this, however, there remains the inescapable question: is uninhibited sex compatible with prodigious accomplishment in thinking and writing, and with keeping operative the supersensitivities of a poet? A young married man on a college faculty, who thrills to Shakespeare's poetry, may have echoed what many young people are thinking when he asked this challenging question: is it coincidence or consequence that during recent years of emancipated sex the world has had no supremely great poet?

Shakespeare does not mince words in describing the conflict within him:

> If eyes, corrupt by over-partial looks,
> Be anchor'd in the bay where all men ride,
> Why of eyes' falsehood hast thou forged hooks,
> Whereto the judgement of my heart is tied?
>
> [Sonnet 137]

It is unlikely that Shakespeare would have let his mistress see such lines as these, which charge her with being accessible to all men, or that he would have bared to her this searching of his conscience. He obviously wrote Sonnet 137 for himself alone and not to be read by her. Indeed, need we suppose that any of the Dark Lady sonnets (except 127, 128, 130, 132, and 145) were intended for her perusal?

With full poignancy the poet describes the abject state to which the intolerable passion for his mistress has reduced him:

> Who taught thee how to make me love thee more,
> The more I hear and see just cause for hate?
>
> [Sonnet 150]

With complete frankness he analyzes himself and unsparingly describes what he finds:

> Love is too young to know what conscience is;
> Yet who knows not conscience is born of love?
> Then, gentle cheater, urge not my amiss,
> Lest guilty of my faults thy sweet self prove;
> For, thou betraying me, I do betray
> My nobler part to my gross body's treason;
> My soul doth tell my body that he may
> Triumph in love; flesh stays no farther reason,
> But rising at thy name doth point out thee
> As his triumphant prize. Proud of this pride,
> He is contented thy poor drudge to be,
> To stand in thy affairs, fall by thy side.
>   No want of conscience hold it that I call
>   Her "love" for whose dear love I rise and fall.
>
> [Sonnet 151]

Though Shakespeare wrote romantic plays, he was himself a frank realist. He was at the opposite pole from a New England Transcendentalist. He was a thoroughgoing experimentalist who observed and recorded his aberrant actions. To his thinking, conscience was not something we have in us when we are born. It was something developed, learned, hammered into us by the consequences of our behavior. Needless to say this view was not expressed in the religious teachings of his day.

He feared weakness, and distrusted spiritual emotions of the kind popularly associated with femininity. In this his "lameness" (Sonnet 81), whatever he means by it, could have been a factor. Some commentators have ascribed these fears to sexual inhibitions which were probably the basic cause of his repressing the feminine side of his personality. However, he does not appear to have been a

75

particularly noteworthy example of sexual insufficiency. He was obviously not a sexual athlete, but neither did he attempt to be one. In Sonnet 138 he speaks of his "age in love" or his having passed the peak of sexual potency, but as we have seen baldly stated in Sonnet 151 there is pride in his potency: "proud of this pride." This phrase should not be unduly stressed, for there is in it no boast. He merely gives it as the reason for his consenting to be a slave to the Dark Lady, her "poor drudge."

The condition to which "sickly appetite" (Sonnet 147) had reduced him is described by him in words applicable to those individuals in each generation who alienate themselves from the values which organized society seeks to maintain:

> My thoughts and my discourse as madmen's are,
> At random from the truth vainly express'd.
>
> [Sonnet 147]

> O me, what eyes hath Love put in my head,
> Which have no correspondence with true sight!
> Or, if they have, where is my judgement fled,
> That censures falsely what they see aright?
> If that be fair whereon my false eyes dote,
> What means the world to say it is not so?
>
> [Sonnet 148]

We cannot call the Dark Lady sonnets more honest than the others, for in all his sonnets Shakespeare faithfully records the experiences through which he attained self-knowledge. The Dark Lady sonnets are a proper ending for self-revelation in regard to his sex life because they tell us, without sidestepping, his personal moral assessment. In Sonnets 147 to 152 we see a man facing himself. In these sonnets Shakespeare has the courage to admit that, in spite of reason and conscience, his "love is as a fever"; he is "past cure" and "frantic-mad with evermore unrest" (Sonnet 147), and is "perjur'd" and "forsworn" (Sonnet 152).

Each reader will decide for himself whether the concluding Sonnets 153 and 154 are, as some think, evidence that Shakespeare acquired a venereal disease from his mistress and went to Bath for a cure; or whether "strange maladies," "sick," "distemper'd," "seething bath," and "healthful remedy for men diseas'd" are figurative expressions referring to spiritual injuries inflicted by Cupid.

The findings in Appendix B enable one to deduce that Shakespeare met his friend after he wrote most of the sonnets to the Dark Lady. The Dark Lady was resident in London, and although the first meeting of the poet and friend occurred after Shakespeare had taken up residence there, it does not necessarily follow that the first meeting was in that city. Indeed, as we shall see, the evidence from the sonnets themselves establishes conclusively that the place of first meeting was in a region remote from the poet's residence—that is remote from London.

In many sonnets the poet tells us he was irresistibly attracted by a lovely boy with "a woman's face" (Sonnet 20), and with hair of an unusual and exquisite color.* He was smitten with the beauty of the young gentleman's eyes. He called the youth "the master-mistress of my passion" (Sonnet 20), and "Lord of my love" (Sonnet 26), and "sweet boy" (Sonnet 108). He said the youth was lovelier than Adonis, than Helen, than the spring (Sonnet 53). He was swept off his feet by this affection, which filled him with lightness of heart. Gone was the sense of desperate loneliness which in youth one needs much courage to face. With assurance that the comforting arms of his friend were around him, ecstasy welled in him, and he wrote:

> Haply I think on thee, and then my state,
> Like to the lark at break of day arising
> From sullen earth, sings hymns at heaven's gate.
> [Sonnet 29]

Finding this friend helped the poet build complete self-confidence and strengthened him against every opposition. In this love he found a safety valve for pent-up uncertainties and anxieties. From the sonnets we deduce that the boy appeared to be—or Shakespeare believed him to be—deeply perceptive of the poet's

---

* "And buds of marjoram had stol'n thy hair." (Sonnet 99). Marjoram is herbaceous, with an aromatic smell. Common or wild marjoram (*Origanum vulgare*) grows in Britain, as does also a somewhat rarer variety, *Origanum aureum*. The latter has golden-yellow flowers. Ingram and Redpath think "buds of marjoram" may refer to sweetness of odor rather than to color.[1] However, the significance of "stol'n" seems to point to color.

77

emotions and inmost thoughts. The boy had a smile that irradiated sympathy and seemed to bespeak thorough understanding. To fulfill his own profound need Shakespeare may have invented in some measure the imaginative understanding which he believed the friend to possess. The poet's ego made it essential that his friend appear unique, a very special and wholly superior person.

The attraction was mutual. At the outset the "beauteous and lovely youth" (Sonnet 54) was enamored of the poet. We surmise that to the boy, perhaps in the audience at some performance in a manor house, the actor and playwright had an aura of glamor about him. In return, the status of the youth as a member of the gentry was socially flattering to the playwright and actor.

It was at a place which was not London, but far from London where Shakespeare toiled at this period of his life, that he first met his friend, or first became aware of the beauty of the young man. Many sonnets make this obvious, but the implications of this fact justify a full demonstration of it.

> My thoughts from far where I abide,
> Intend a zealous pilgrimage to thee.
>
> [Sonnet 27]

> How far I toil, still farther off from thee.
>
> [Sonnet 28]

In Sonnet 39 we are told that the poet and the friend "divided live," and that the poet deplores "this separation."

There is much more of the same:

> If the dull substance of my flesh were thought,
> Injurious distance should not stop my way;
> For then, despite of space, I would be brought,
> From limits far remote, where thou dost stay.
>
> [Sonnet 44]

> "Thus far the miles are measur'd from my friend!"
>
> [Sonnet 50]

> From where thou art why should I haste me thence?
> Till I return, of posting is no need. . . .
> Then can no horse with my desire keep pace.
>
> [Sonnet 51]

Is it thy spirit that thou send'st from thee
So far from home into my deeds to pry.

[Sonnet 61]

That the friend's home was far from London is further supported by other sonnets, and by the discovery (see Chapter 14) that
the name of the friend Shakespeare planted in the sonnets is that of
a man who has been identified as a Lancashire youth.

After the first meeting, Shakespeare travels away from the
friend (Sonnet 50). He is writing plays without having yet achieved
any success which the friend could "recite" of him as "merit"
(Sonnet 72). Ingram and Redpath think it most likely that Sonnet
72 refers to Shakespeare's being under "the social stigma of being a
writer for the public playhouse"—ostensibly before his playwriting
had brought him honor. Toiling in comparative poverty, quivering
from enforced contact with vulgarity, and depressed by the feeling
that his is a "slight Muse" (Sonnet 38), he thinks of what some men
possess: high birth, skill, wealth, body's force, fine garments, hawks
and hounds, and fine horses. These he repudiates:

But these particulars are not my measure;
All these I better in one general best.

[Sonnet 91]

He finds compensation in the love of his friend.

It seems obvious that Shakespeare penned a considerable
number of his sonnets to his friend while he himself was on the low
rung of the ladder. Only before he achieved recognition as a playwright does it seem likely that he could have written:

When, in disgrace with fortune and men's eyes,
I all alone beweep my outcast state.

[Sonnet 29]

or

Now, while the world is bent my deeds to cross.

[Sonnet 90]

Sonnet 90, which speaks of "a purpos'd overthrow," seems to
express the poet's reaction to a severe attack upon the kind of
writing he was doing in 1589.

79

4*

Shakespeare also speaks of lameness:

> So I, made lame by Fortune's dearest spite.
>
> [Sonnet 37]

While some believe he means physical lameness, it is far more likely lameness of another kind. Physical lameness in him as an actor on the stage would in all probability have given rise to a tradition of it. If his lameness is metaphorical, as it probably is, then we must ask to what stylistic, literary, emotional, or mental lameness it refers. If metaphorical, it would seem to apply to some time before he had begun to achieve a large success on the London stage and before he was generally looked upon as not "lame, poor, nor despis'd" (Sonnet 37). In Sonnet 89, "speak of my lameness, and I straight will halt," clearly implies that "he is not lame, but would be willing to limp as if he were—should it be his friend's caprice to accuse him of any disability. All he cares about is his friend's opinion of him."[2]

Within a year or two after the first meeting, the friend visits London. The friend's beauty attracts general attention among Shakespeare's acquaintances in the city, and several in "their poesy" are inspired thereby. Sonnet 78 speaks of "every alien pen" that sings of the friend, and how "in others' works" the effect of the friend's beauty serves to "mend the style." In Sonnet 79 Shakespeare admits to the friend that his beauty deserves "a worthier pen" than his own. He says that such a new admirer is now praising the friend in verse:

> And my sick Muse doth give another place.
>
> [Sonnet 79]

As a compliment to the friend, but with what amounts almost to a jealous and belittling comment on the capacity of the other poet, Shakespeare says it is only because of the friend's virtuous behavior and beauty that the other poet has subject matter for his praise. Sonnets 80 to 85 show that Shakespeare feels envious of one rival poet in particular, whom he describes as "a better spirit," a "golden quill," and "that able spirit . . . in polish'd form of well refined pen." Sonnet 86 makes it appear that this rival poet could have been

Christopher Marlowe. Some phrases in it seem definitely applicable to Marlowe: "the proud full sail of his great verse," "his spirit, by spirits taught to write above a mortal pitch," and "his compeers by night giving him aid." The word "night" could be a reference to the School of Night, whose scholars pursued Natural Philosophy, in which subject knowledge was dangerous because it was considered heretical by the populace. For this reason the scholars of the School of Night held their meetings and discussions in secret. Marlowe, as a government spy, is believed to have been associated with those scholars. The phrase, "that affable familiar ghost which nightly gulls him with intelligence" could refer to someone else—perhaps a literary man who sold Marlowe unreliable information. On the other hand, Ingram and Redpath think the rival poet could have been George Chapman. They present cogent arguments (in a note to Sonnet 86), but their explanation of the double reference to "Night" would require a dating after the publication of Chapman's *The Shadow of Night* in 1594. Open-line percentages and syllabic intensity point to some year definitely earlier than that as the date of the friend's visit to London.

In the first eleven lines of Sonnet 86 Shakespeare describes the other poet's rivalry, presumably as a dramatist, and then concludes:

> I was not sick of any fear from thence:
> But when your countenance fill'd up his line,
> Then lack'd I matter; that enfeebl'd mine.

He soon had cause for greater suffering. When he introduced his friend to his mistress, the friend aroused Shakespeare's jealousy by becoming one of her lovers. Fearful of losing his friend, Shakespeare was reduced to clinging to a thin thread: "we must not be foes" (Sonnet 40).

The friend returned to his distant home. After his departure Shakespeare grieved:

> But ah, thought kills me, that I am not thought,
> To leap large lengths of miles when thou art gone.
> [Sonnet 44]

During both periods of their separation—before and after the friend's visit to London—there was communication back and forth

(Sonnet 45). In the course of time Shakespeare probably sent more of his sonnets to the friend than cool reason would have found advisable. They were in all respects uninhibited love letters.

Time as well as distance separated the two. Sonnets 97 and 98 are evidence of the passage of considerable time during which the poet and friend have not seen each other.

It seems clear from Sonnet 100 that for at least several months in 1593 while composing *The Rape of Lucrece*, no sonnets to the friend or inspired by him came from Shakespeare's pen.

> Where art thou, Muse, that thou forget'st so long
> To speak of that which gives thee all thy might?
> Spend'st thou thy fury on some worthless song,
> Darkening thy power to lend base subjects light?
> Return, forgetful Muse, and straight redeem
> In gentle numbers time so idly spent;
> Sing to the ear that doth thy lays esteem
> And gives thy pen both skill and argument.
> Rise, resty Muse, my love's sweet face survey,
> If Time have any wrinkle graven there.
>
> [Sonnet 100]

The Muse's "fury" is comparable to the intensity of tone in *The Rape of Lucrece*. The phrase "lend base subjects light" reminds us of line 674 in *The Rape*: "light and lust are deadly enemies." The phrase "time so idly spent" is reminiscent of the promise Shakespeare had made in the dedications of *Venus and Adonis* to use "all idle hours" in writing the second narrative poem. The last two lines quoted from that sonnet are a clear indication that a long time has passed since the poet has seen the face of the friend.

Further, of Sonnet 83, Ingram and Redpath say: "It seems as if the first quatrain refers to a time when Shakespeare wrote about his friend . . . whereas the second quatrain refers to a recent period of silence."

About 1596 Shakespeare wrote Sonnets 1 to 17, urging his friend to marry. C. S. Lewis feels this urging is "not consistent with normal friendship" and he asks: "What man in the whole world, except a father or a potential father-in-law, cares whether any other man gets married?"[3]

Several years older than his friend (Sonnet 22), Shakespeare by

82

1596 had acquired something of the affection of a father toward the younger man "most rich in youth" (Sonnet 15). The difference in age (about seven years—see Chapter 14) between poet and friend are basic to all interpretations of the story in the *Sonnets*. However, the death of Shakespeare's ten-year-old son Hamnet in August 1596 may also have been a factor in the poet's urging his friend to marry and beget a son (Sonnet 13).

11

TO THE EDGE OF DOOM

"'Fair, kind, and true,' is all my argument."

SONNET 105

W HETHER OR NOT WE ARE WILLING TO ADMIT IT, all of us have unconventional sexual impulses of kinds not permissible to indulge. No one completely eradicates these animal cravings. Although society frowns on them and the person himself disapproves, every one of us is predisposed to some degree of neurosis. In plain Shakespearean language, Shakespeare's problem was one we all meet.

His infatuation with this male friend began with lightheartedness. It gave joy and ecstasy. It seems clear that the poet thought of the friendship—or aimed to make it—of the kind advocated by Spenser in the Glosse to the first eclogue in the *Shepherd's Calendar*:

Hobbinol is a fained country name, whereby, it being so commune and usuall, seemeth to be hidden the person of some his very speciall and most familiar friend, whom he entirely and extraordinarily beloved, as peradventure shall be more largely declared hereafter. In thys place seemeth to be some savour of disorderly love, which the learned call *paederastice*: but it is gathered beside his meaning. For who that hath red Plato his dialogue called Alcybiades, Zenophon, and Maximus Tyrius, of Socrates opinions, may easily perceive that such love is muche to be alowed and liked of, specially so meant as Socrates used it: who sayeth, that in deede he loved Alcybiades extremely, yet not Alcybiades person, but hys soule, which is Alcybiades owne selfe. And so is *paederastice* much to be preferred before *gynerastice* that is, the love which enflameth man with lust toward womankind. But yet let no man thinke, that herein I stand with Lucian, or his develish disciple Unico Aretino, in defence of execrable and horrible sinnes of forbidden and unlawful fleshlinesse.*

A Princeton professor, Henry McClure Young, maintains that the passion Shakespeare felt for his friend did not become an affair of physical homosexuality.[2] A psychologist, Harold Grier McCurdy, is of the same opinion.[3] George W. Knight says Shakespeare's sonnets are "sexually impregnated" and "burning with sexual, or homosexual passion, yet chaste."[4]

Against such tender pleading one might argue from Sonnet 35, in which Shakespeare speaks of the friend's "trespass" and "sensual fault." The poet finds "such civil war" in his own love and hate, that he "an accessary needs must be" and he declares in Sonnet 36:

> In our two loves there is but one respect . . .
> Which though it alter not love's sole effect,
> Yet doth it steal sweet hours from love's delight.
> I may not evermore acknowledge thee,
> Lest my bewailed guilt should do thee shame,
> Nor thou with public kindness honour me,
> Unless thou take that honour from thy name.

In the relationship between poet and friend before the triangle situation arose, there entered a sense of guilt. This led to the poet's

* In 1533–34 sodomy was made a felony. This act was repealed in 1547, but in 1548 it was again provided that the offense should be a felony. It was repealed in 1553, but in 1562–63 a statue of King Henry VIII was revived and made it perpetual.[1]

feeling that the two must part and their names not be associated, in order to save reputations, or avoid catastrophe.

However intimate their relationship at first flush, it did not continue as an affair of physical homosexuality. There is a sonnet that makes this absolutely clear. After whatever discovery of physical passion there may have been, Shakespeare repudiates the desire to possess the body of his "master-mistress," and this is because the friend is a male:

> A man in hue, all hues in his controlling,
> Which steals men's eyes and women's souls amazeth.
> And for a woman wert thou first created;
> Till Nature, as she wrought thee, fell a-doting,
> And by addition me of thee defeated,
> By adding one thing to my purpose nothing.
> > But since she pricked thee out for women's pleasure,
> > Mine be thy love, and thy love's use their treasure.
> > > [Sonnet 20]

Homosexuals cannot claim that Shakespeare was like themselves.

Shakespeare is not enigmatic. *The Two Gentlemen of Verona*, written during the period in which he was writing the bulk of the sonnets to the friend, is, of all his plays, the one that echoes most closely phrases and turns of thought in the sonnets. It deals with a love between two men that is based upon their mutual assumption that the love of man for woman cannot rival in strength and preciousness their love for each other. Valentine and Proteus place friendship between men on a higher plane than the unavoidably sexual love of man for woman. But Proteus falls in love with Julia. Valentine sees this as a "folly." Then we find that Valentine has been mastered by the same folly in his love for Silvia. Complications arise. Proteus treacherously shifts affection from Julia to Silvia. Although the love between the two men remains strong enough to cause Proteus to repent with incredible swiftness and Valentine to forgive him with equally incredible speed, Shakespeare ends the play by having the two friends marry women.

Many sonnets to the friend are suffused with the rapture which the love at first gives. While he suffers intense distress from the first parting and from subsequent separation by distance (Sonnet 27),   87 the lonely poet in London sings of gladness and exultation in such sonnets as 29, 52, and 91.

The impassioned friendship unavoidably brings the poet agonies of spirit. He feels with sadness the impermanence of beauty. He grieves in realizing in retrospect that the perfection of the initial relationship with his friend had been of brief duration—"but one hour mine" (Sonnet 33). With somber thoughts of aging and death, he decries the effect of Time upon himself in Sonnets 22, 62, 73, and 74. In Sonnet 104 he maintains that three years in their passing have not stolen any beauty from his young friend. "To me, fair friend, you never can be old." But he fears that there may have been changes of which he is not fully aware, and he says, "mine eye may be deceived." In Sonnets 60, 64, and 65 he bewails the inevitable march of Time, and laments that Time ultimately spoils beauty.

Against this brooding on the decay and death of all loveliness, he takes comfort in the thought that his love for his friend is eternal. It must be, on two counts: he himself will never cease to love the friend, and his love for his friend will forever shine bright "in black ink"—in the verse which he confidently claims will give it immortality so long as the human race endures.

After the initial separation by distance, there comes a worse separation of another kind. The friend visits London, but inflicts deepest agony upon the poet when with "lascivious grace" he attracts the attention of the Dark Lady (Sonnet 40). She woos the youth, and the two together "break a twofold truth":

> Hers, by thy beauty tempting her to thee,
> Thine, by thy beauty being false to me.
>
> [Sonnet 41]

The poet is tortured not only by jealousy of the friend and the mistress, but by jealousy of another poet who has become inspired by the friend's beauty. While he is apprehensive lest the flattering attention of the other poet wean his friend away, his chief fear is that the Dark Lady, in granting the boy her favors, has lost the poet his friend forever:

> Farewell! thou art too dear for my possessing.
>
> [Sonnet 87]

And he is plagued by doubts as to the friend's reaction to himself:

> Thou mayst be false, and yet I know it not.
>
> [Sonnet 92]

Even so, in his loneliness he clings to a conviction which above everything his ego must maintain, that the friend's love for him is essentially unchanged:

> So shall I live, supposing thou art true,
> Like a deceived husband; so love's face
> May still seem love to me, though alter'd new.
>
> [Sonnet 93]

He winces at the fact that the friend makes love to the Dark Lady in his "sport" (Sonnet 95), and he assails the friend with accusations:

> Lilies that fester smell far worse than weeds.
>
> [Sonnet 94]

> O, what a mansion have those vices got
> Which for their habitation chose out thee!
>
> [Sonnet 95]

> Some say, thy fault is youth, some wantonness.
>
> [Sonnet 96]

Sonnet 120 may refer to an initial intimacy, or to the occasion when the poet introduced the youth to the Dark Lady. To either of these, the expressions in that sonnet seem applicable: "our night of woe," "my transgression," "your crime," "wounded bosoms," and "your trespass" and "mine."

He reproaches his mistress:

> Of him, myself, and thee, I am forsaken.
>
> [Sonnet 133]

In despair he cries out:

> Him have I lost; thou hast both him and me.
>
> [Sonnet 134]

To avoid having to admit to certainty, he professes uncertainty   89 as to how much the friend and mistress mean to each other, but he voices his suspicions:

> To win me soon to hell, my female evil
> Tempteth my better angel from my side,
> And would corrupt my saint to be a devil,
> Wooing his purity with her foul pride.
> And whether that my angel be turn'd fiend
> Suspect I may, yet not directly tell;
> But being both from me, both to each friend,
> I guess one angel in another's hell.

[Sonnet 144]

The poet-mistress-boy triangle yields insights into irrationality. Shakespeare's love for the Dark Lady is against all reason, and so also, we suspect, is his love for the young friend. He states no fully adequate reason for that love. Love, of course, needs no reason. Yet it is pertinent to ask why such a poet as Shakespeare finds great worth in the friend. What is the basis of his high esteem? The poet's affection was not directed primarily toward the friend's body, or so he told himself (Sonnet 20). If it was not the boy's body, what was it? Does the poet love anything beside beauty of face and form in the youth? The youth's smile, we surmise, communicates a look of sympathy and an illusion of deep understanding. Is the basis of the poet's affection the youth's character? Hardly. Shakespeare is forced to seek an excuse for the boy's behavior. Is it, then, the boy's mind? Never once does the poet make us feel that he has been stimulated by the youth's intelligence, nor does he give us any evidence that the friend is particularly mature or articulate. Shakespeare tells us that the friend is not a poet: "I grant thou wert not married to my Muse" (Sonnet 82). All we know of the reason for Shakespeare's love is that there is, or he believes there is, mutual affection. The friend sends him writing tablets—a thoughtful gift—or an obvious one. Nothing told us about the youth warrants the extreme value placed upon him. We cannot avoid being impressed by what Shakespeare fails to specify. When forced to admit flaws in the youth, he is left with a desperate determination to continue loving. This appears to be a requirement of his ego. William Shakespeare must have it that his beloved is a person who deserves immortality.

90   It is his will to immortalize his friend, but he gives only one

clear reason why he should: that the friend has inspired his sonnet-eering. Thus, turning inward, he finds in his own poetry a value to compensate for what he presumably does not find in the friend. The poet extols his own work, his art. In writing his sonnets, Shakespeare triumphs over any inadequacies he may have felt in himself, and surmounts every external loss. It may be that the wellspring of all art is an impulse to compensate for a feeling of inferiority. If so, what more satisfying success, what more perfect fulfillment, can any human being achieve?

The nearest to a hint of Shakespeare's estimation of the friend's worth is his feeling that the friend is an appreciative reader of the sonnets addressed to him. This is why the poet, after a period during which he has not written any sonnets, admonishes himself for the lapse and decides to resume writing sonnets to the friend (Sonnet 100).

We see clearly how two points of the triangle affect Shakespeare in his tortured corner of it. What may not be so obvious is that the two loves validate each other. The poet's love for his mistress gives proper perspective to his love for the boy. He can forgive the boy for sporting in sex because he cannot overcome it in himself. Without the sonnets to the Dark Lady, the sonnets to the friend would stand impeached. Without the sonnets to the friend, the sonnets to the mistress would be intolerable. Each section is essential to our acceptance of the other. The interplay of the two makes a work of art superior to what either would be alone.

In the sonnets the lark rises with song that will be heard repeatedly in the same accents throughout the poet's career. Experiences described in the sonnets prepare Shakespeare for delineating self-defeating characters from Tarquin to Troilus. He learns that we bring tragedy upon ourselves through those we love, and this he will show in many lovers: Romeo, Hamlet, Othello, Lear, Antony. Like himself in the sonnets, he will show Hamlet and Othello shattered by belief in their beloved's falseness. He loses faith in his friend, but persuades himself that his trust in him will preserve the friend's affection, just as Troilus will think his confidence in Cressida will preserve hers.

In general appraisal we note that the sonnets show Shakespeare defiant of convention and impelled to question society's concepts of good and evil:

91

> Most true it is that I have look'd on truth
> Askance and strangely.
>
> [Sonnet 110]

His self-analysis is unsparing:

> What potions have I drunk of Siren tears,
> Distill'd from limbecks foul as hell within,
> Applying fears to hopes and hopes to fears,
> Still losing when I saw myself to win!
> What wretched errors hath my heart committed, . . .
> In the distraction of this madding fever!
>
> [Sonnet 119]

Sonnet 121, which is the most penetrating of all in its self-revelation, seems to show indebtedness to Montaigne, whose essays Shakespeare may have read in Florio's translation. While Shakespeare had a strong sense of social propriety, he set a higher value on something else:

> 'Tis better to be vile than vile esteemed,
> When not to be receives reproach of being;
> And the just pleasure lost, which is so deemed
> Not by our feeling, but by others' seeing:
> For why should others' false adulterate eyes
> Give salutation to my sportive blood?
> Or on my frailties why are frailer spies,
> Which in their wills count bad what I think good?
> No, I am that I am, and they that level
> At my abuses reckon up their own:
> I may be straight though they themselves be bevel.

The sonnets give voice to a deep-rooted instinct. They also show that the index to a man's character is not what he feels, and not so much what he does as the goal toward which he strives. Here enters what Robert Ardrey in *African Genesis* calls "the mighty paradox." While human thought finds itself incapable of imprisoning an animal instinct, human thought is never imprisoned by an animal instinct.[5] Imagination is free. In addition to detailing Shakespeare's struggle against animal instincts, the free and actively creating mind of the poet gives an important contribution to humanity's struggle to harmonize physical and intellectual and spiritual love. In part, I believe, he effected this by the conscious artistry in which he arranged the order of his sonnets for publication.

As no poet before or since, Shakespeare came to grips with the perplexing problems of human relationships. His sonnets affirmed that the misdirection of sex runs counter to love. He announced his discovery:

> Now I find true
> That better is by evil still made better,
> And ruin'd love, when it is built anew,
> Grows fairer than at first, more strong, far greater.
>
> [Sonnet 119]

With a sensitivity to beauty and spiritual values excelled by no other poet, he affirmed what he had learned from experience, that ideal love belongs in physical marriage. He said this directly in the first seventeen sonnets. He said it indirectly throughout all the sonnets. He declared for love in marriage in *The Two Gentlemen of Verona* and in thirty plays thereafter.

Instructed by the self-knowledge which the sonnets show he had acquired, Shakespeare could later put into the mouth of one and the same person: "I could accuse me of such things that it were better my mother had not born me," and "What a piece of work is man! How noble in reason! how infinite in faculties!"

In facing the duality of man's nature, the poet learned that spiritual love triumphant over preoccupation with bodily desire is a goal never fully reached. His sonnets are the supreme expression of human will striving toward that goal.

In many sonnets he attains heights of affirmation in asserting that love as something more than physical passion not only does exist but can be permanent, or rather, is permanent. In Sonnet 115 he affirms that such love continues to grow. In one of the most eloquent of the sonnets he says:

> Let me not to the marriage of true minds
> Admit impediments. Love is not love
> Which alters when it alteration finds, . . .
> O, no! it is an ever-fixed mark,
> That looks on tempests and is never shaken;

93

It is the star to every wandering bark, . . .
Love's not Time's fool, though rosy lips and cheeks
Within his bending sickle's compass come;
Love alters not with his brief hours and weeks,
But bears it out even to the edge of doom.

[Sonnet 116]

The subject matter of the sonnets is an interweaving of two elements: self-knowledge and truths of universal applicability. The affirmations are elaborations of the "three themes in one" of which Shakespeare says:

"Fair, kind, and true," is all my argument.

[Sonnet 105]

This is the nearest the poet comes to formulating a personal philosophy. Included in the meaning of "fair" is beauty. "Kind" means having the goodness of affection, a feeling of kinship. As for "true," we partly sense his meaning in his use of the term "true minds" (Sonnet 116), by which in contrast with all else, we judge that he means minds that attempt to face reality beneath all self-deceptions. We sense his further meaning in the use of "a true soul" (Sonnet 125). Here the concept is of a love transcending all blows of circumstance that tend to destroy it.

In the sonnets the poet expresses ecstasy, lonesomeness, abject despair, self-condemnation, a glorying in friendship, unquestioning trust, shock of disillusionment, suspicion, jealousy, hatred, a love resigned to lack of reciprocal affection, a love that survives all losses and asks nothing in return, a more unselfish love than any poet had ever voiced. In this connection, C. S. Lewis makes a most perceptive statement: "Shakespeare ends by expressing simply love, the quintessence of all loves. . . . The greatest of the sonnets are written from a region in which love abandons all claims and flowers into charity. . . . This patience, this anxiety (more like a parent's than a lover's) to find excuses for the beloved, this clear-sighted and wholly unembittered resignation, this transference of the whole self into another self without the demand for a return, have hardly a precedent in profane literature."[6]

Through the experiences recorded in his sonnets, Shakespeare

94

grew to an understanding of love and was able to put into the mouth of the shepherd Silvius in the Forest of Arden the wise and moving words which we feel are from the poet's own heart:

> Tell this youth what 'tis to love.
> It is to be all made of sighs and tears; ...
> It is to be all made of faith and service; ...
> It is to be all made of fantasy,
> All made of passion and all made of wishes;
> All adoration, duty, and observance,
> All humbleness, all patience, and impatience,
> All purity, all trial, all obeisance.
> [*As You Like It*, 5.2.90–105]

12

BARREN OF NEW PRIDE

"Thou art all my art."

SONNET 78

MANY OF SHAKESPEARE'S SONNETS ARE TECHNICALLY perfect. Their author certainly worked and reworked some of them painstakingly. This we see from comparison of the *Passionate Pilgrim* sonnets 1, 2, 3, and 5 with their subsequent reappearance in Sonnets 138 and 144, and in *Love's Labour's Lost*, 4.3.60 and 4.2.110. These four constitute direct evidence from the poet's writing table of his alertness in self-criticism and his thoughtful revamping and repolishing.* Further, they testify that their

---

* In verses prefacing the First Folio, Ben Jonson tells us that Shakespeare not only expressed "Nature" (wrote with naturalness) but also labored at his Art:

> My gentle Shakespeare, . . . he,
> Who casts to write a living line, must sweat,
>   (Such as thine are) and strike the second heat
> Upon the Muses' anvil; turn the same,
>   (And himself with it) that he thinks to frame;
> Or for the laurel, he may gain a scorn,
>   For a great Poet's made, as well as born·
> And such wert thou.

Passionate Pilgrim versions were earlier compositions. No one who analyzes these versions can believe that the order of composition was the reverse.

The improvements, one of them a completely new eighth line when *Passionate Pilgrim* No. 1 became Sonnet 138, are in the direction of greater clarity and meaningfulness. Note the greater maturity in lines 4, 11, and 14 of "unlearned . . . in subtleties" as against "unskilful . . . in forgeries," and the superiority, in the context, of "seeming trust" to "soothing tongue" and "flatter'd" to "smother'd."

In the first edition of 1609, in Sonnet 144, line 6, "sight" is believed to have been a compositor's error. Most editors amend it to "side," used in *Passionate Pilgrim* No. 2, because it gives a more satisfactory rhyme and sense. But in their notes on Sonnet 144, Ingram and Redpath mention several other instances in which Sonnet 144 has improvements over *Passionate Pilgrim* No. 2.

In the whole sequence of the sonnets, more than forty are paired in subject matter. Where there is pairing, the first sonnet usually seems more concrete, more directly from objective experience; the second seems more mentally spun.

Sonnet 99 begins with an extra line which is essential to understanding. The octave and sestet are not intelligible without that introductory line. Sonnet 126 is what would be commonly called imperfect for it has only twelve lines and is couplet-rhymed.

In the sonnets to his friend the poet makes many references to his own style. In this connection, observe a statement by Gascoigne:

> Stand most upon the excellencie of your Invention. . . . For that being founde, pleasant wordes will follow well inough and fast inough.

Gascoigne is saying that where there is excellent subject matter, verses will flow easily. Whether or not Shakespeare has Gascoigne's statement in mind, he writes the following which sounds like an echo of Gascoigne:

> How can my Muse want subject to invent,
> While thou dost breathe, that pour'st into my verse
> Thine own sweet argument, . . .
> For who's so dumb that cannot write to thee,
> When thou thyself dost give invention light?

[Sonnet 38]

The poet is very conscious of the effect his affection for his friend has upon his verse style:

> Why is my verse so barren of new pride,
> So far from variation or quick change?
> Why with the time do I not glance aside
> To new-found methods and to compounds strange?
> Why write I still all one, ever the same,
> And keep invention in a noted weed,
> That every word doth almost tell my name,
> Showing their birth and where they did proceed?
>
> [Sonnet 76]

Love for the friend overcomes the handicap of having had less formal education than most of the other poets in London. Love for the friend plays a major part in shaping the warm eloquence and the quality we recognize as Shakespearean "in every word . . . almost" which our poet writes.

He says to the friend:

> be most proud of that which I compile,
> Whose influence is thine and born of thee:
> In others' works thou dost but mend the style,
> And arts with thy sweet graces graced be;
> But thou art all my art, and dost advance
> As high as learning my rude ignorance.
>
> [Sonnet 78]

Because all Shakespeare's works testify to his great poetic sensitivity, we can be sure that he would not say what he does about following his own way had he not already developed an established style by the time he came to writing the sonnets to the friend. Though aware that his style is unique, rather than describe it, he tells what it is not. It is not like that of any rival playwright. He does not think of himself as a progressive moving with the *avant-garde* but as an outsider steering his own course. He refuses to follow the trend of London fashion in verse, undoubtedly sensing that fashion is the enemy of poetry—that it is a form of self-defense used by those who are too uncertain of themselves to dare to stand alone. His style through the years is not always the same, unchanging, but his

99

personal touch is always in it, like a man's face that changes as he grows older, yet remains recognizably his. Shakespeare's style develops, but in his manner, not anyone else's. He is a solitary lark.

While he refers frequently to his own verse style in the sonnets to his friend, he makes no reference to his style in the sonnets to the Dark Lady. His sonnets testify that from 1589 love gave him so much to say he does not need to embellish them with artifice or with any of the latest literary devices. His love for his friend constantly renews his inspiration, "as the sun is daily new." In Sonnet 76 he says to his friend: "You and love are still my argument."

Not only the love but all its unhappy consequences are material for his pen. It seems that with at least part of his mind he relishes all the triangle miseries including jealousy and sense of loss, because he is making copy out of every emotion. He is a sensitive and demanding lover, but a more sensitive and demanding poet.

When he refers to the poetry of others who are inspired by the beauty of his friend, especially the poetry of that other Muse who may have been Marlowe (Sonnet 86)—that "better spirit" who wrote of his friend—Shakespeare describes himself as "tongue-tied" (Sonnet 80), a "sick Muse" (Sonnet 79). He calls his own verse a "saucy bark, inferior far to his" (Sonnet 80). This self-depreciation is exaggerated, but not so his humble gratitude for the effect his friend's love has upon his writing. We agree with him when, in contrast with the other Muse's "great verse" (Sonnet 86), he describes his own as "my gentle verse" (Sonnet 81). Yet in Sonnet 81 he also repudiates self-depreciation and does not hesitate to assert with aplomb and an almost audacious confidence that his verse will confer "immortal life" upon his friend—"such virtue hath my pen."

There seems to be no doubt that his complacency in regard to his own style was rudely shaken by the sharp attack Thomas Nash made on the stylistic excesses committed by a playwright Nash called a "mediocritie." This attack by Nash in his "Prefix" to Robert Greene's *Menaphon*, was published in the midsummer of 1589. Our Chapter 8 shows that Nash's "Prefix" is applicable to passages in a play Shakespeare wrote. The critical arrows could not have failed to wound a poet as sensitive as Shakespeare. A sonnet which speaks of a great storm of "spite" which had blown against him seems biographically significant:

Then hate me when thou wilt; if ever, now;
Now, while the world is bent my deeds to cross,
Join with the spite of fortune, make me bow,
And do not drop in for an after-loss;
Ah, do not, when my heart hath 'scaped this sorrow,
Come in the rearward of a conquer'd woe;
Give not a windy night a rainy morrow,
To linger out a purposed overthrow.

[Sonnet 90]

In appraisal of the quality of verse in the sonnets, the "correct" view has been that they are consistently of a high order of poetry. In consequence, few have had the temerity to assert otherwise. Arthur Lynch said in 1919: "The fact that many of the Sonnets are devoid of poetic value has been timidly suggested by Gervinus, but George Wyndham trounces him."[1] M. M. Mahood, writing in 1937, may need help from heaven; for while she says that some of the sonnets "cry with the voice of true feeling," she ventures to say of others, "their tortuous artifice makes them poor poems."[2]

It seems fair to say that some of the sonnets are not extraordinary poems, but all lovers of poetry agree that many are among the greatest poems in the English language. Practically all of them make us feel they were composed at white heat, or red heat, in the course of the emotional experience related. While some of them, like Sonnet 30, are recollections in tranquillity, Mahood thinks that when Shakespeare wrote most of his sonnets he was "not sufficiently detached from the experience that gave rise to them to be able to watch all the forces of his mind at play. . . . Shakespeare's feelings about his friend are for the most part too confused to make a shapely sonnet. . . . In only a few of the poems addressed to the youth are these stored experiences ordered into a work of art."[3]

To the contrary, we should note that the warmth with which the poet expresses his love is often so exciting that it obscures our realization of the artistry. There is also a reciprocal effect. Shakespeare's artistry intensifies his love. His giving voice to his love deepened it, renewed its force, kept it alive: "Ten times happy me!" (Sonnet 37); "So are you to my thoughts as food to life" (Sonnet 75); "My verse alone had all thy gentle grace" (Sonnet 79). He observes that out of the death of roses "are sweetest odours made," and so he tells the "beauteous and lovely youth" that the essence of   101

his perfection will be preserved: "When that shall vade (fade?),*
by (my?)* verse distils your truth" (Sonnet 54).

It has been said that to understand Shakespeare's sonnets it is
necessary to have read many of the sonnets of his contemporaries.

Many Elizabethan sonnets were written by the so-called Vogue
sonneteers.† The Vogue sonnets exaggerate the extravagance of the
Petrarchan mode; they subordinate passion to conceits; their
writers pass as lovers suffering the extremity of romantic love, but
they seldom communicate a conviction of sincerity. They pursue a
highly conventional pattern in mood and intention.

Those of us who have read many of the Vogue sonnets agree
that the typical Elizabethan sonneteer, when raving of the girl he
swears he loves, is more in love with his own creative imagination
than with the girl. We cannot put the sonneteering Shakespeare into
their category. To argue that he invented his mistress and his friend
and his affection for both, and thus engaged in what was merely a
literary exercise, would contradict every impression his sonnets give
us. It would emasculate these poems. The theory that he created the
Dark Lady and his friend is untenable from every angle.

If the poet had created the friend, he would have employed
verisimilitude to enable us to visualize him. He would have described the boy's gestures, mannerisms, costume, and so forth.
Instead he does not even describe the youth's beauty, except to give
a probable hint as to the color of the young man's hair. There is
nothing to disturb our impression that the friend was a real person
whose identity Shakespeare was at the time meticulously concealing.
The poet himself warns us against making the mistake of thinking
that he invented his friend:

> Who will believe my verse in time to come,
> If it were fill'd with your most high deserts? . . .
> If I could write the beauty of your eyes
> And in fresh numbers number all your graces,
> The age to come would say. "This poet lies;
> Such heavenly touches ne'er touch'd earthly faces."
>
> [Sonnet 17]

* For two hundred years Shakespearean scholars have been divided as to
whether the words should be *vade* or *fade*, and *by* or *my*.

† The first published sequence in the Vogue type was Thomas Watson's
Hecatompathia, 1582. Although this was of eighteen-line stanzas, the Vogue pattern
was there.

As actor and playwright, Shakespeare understood supremely well the technique of characterizing a person by the effect he has on others. We become acquainted with the young friend through the effect he has on Shakespeare and the extent to which he is the "begetter" of the sonnets. At the same time, we are shown that effect, we are presented with the dramatist's greatest characterization—greater than Falstaff or Hamlet—himself, William Shakespeare.

All the poet's protestation notwithstanding, Shakespeare was less interested in the friend than in himself. This does not in any degree belittle the love he felt for his friend. Rather it enhances it. A generation after Shakespeare's, the poet Lovelace said: "I could not love thee, dear, so much, lov'd I not honour more." The only person capable of the greatest love for another is one who sets the highest value on his own integrity.

When some of Shakespeare's sonnets were distributed among his friends, and all later published, the poet was ignoring his own statement:

> That love is merchandized whose rich esteeming
> The owner's tongue doth publish every where.
> [Sonnet 102]

But with publication and the reaction of readers, individual sonnets began to rub against each other, throwing new light on each other and their author. Some of them became more than what the poet had felt at the moment of writing, and they began to pulsate with emotions and meanings brought to them by their readers. They entered into a process of socialization, and so also did the poet through them. In individual sonnets he gave voice to profound personal problems stemming from lust, homosexual impulse, jealousy, and so forth. His self-purging exposed these problems and himself to the eyes of all men. Publication of his sonnets was essential for Shakespeare's personal fulfillment, as he no doubt realized.

While some of his sonnets are not supremely great poems—though some are—the whole sequence is a transcending work of art. It is a social communication, presenting the poet's deepest personal involvements. Vibrant with emotions and meanings which it awakens in us, it speaks profoundly to everyone.

103

5

13

SHAKE-SCENE

"to critic and to flatterer."

SONNET 112

A PAMPHLET, *A Groats-worth of Witte, bought with a Million of Repentence*, was entered for publication on September 20, 1592, as the work of Robert Greene, who had died on September 2. Warren B. Austin suggests that it may have been a literary impersonation written in two weeks by Henry Chettle to satisfy a "publisher's demand for sensational copy." What facts we have would seem to allow, though they do not prove, Chettle authorship. Whether *A Groats-worth* was by Greene or Chettle is, however of little concern. What is important is how it touched Shakespeare; in what ways, if at all, it affected his career. In it was an attack upon Marlowe, a seemingly direct result of which was the elimination of two of our playwright's contemporaries:

> Wonder not (for with thee will I first begin) thou famous gracer of tragedies, that Greene, who hath said like thee (like the fool in his

heart), "there is no God," should now give glory unto His greatness; for penetrating is his power, his hand lies heavy upon me. . . . He is a God that can punish enemies. Why should thy excellent wit, His Gift, be so blinded that thou should'st give no Glory to the Giver? It is a pestilent Machiavellian policy that thou hast studied? . . . I know the least of my demerits merit this miserable death, but wilful striving against known truth exceedeth all the terrors of my soul. . . . Defer not, with me, till this last point of extremity; for little knowest thou how in the end thou shalt be visited.

In view of the sixteenth century's frenetic horror of atheists, who were held to be hated by God, the assertion that Marlowe denied a belief in God was an extremely grave condemnation. Coming as a deathbed testimony by one who had known Marlowe intimately, the accusation was widely accepted as true. While Marlowe seems to have privately and unwisely jested at the Scriptures, he might have survived to learn caution, had not his dying acquaintance marked him as a man under God's curse. When in 1593 an atheistical document was found affixed to a church wall, Marlowe was suspected of having written it. Thomas Kyd, who had at one time roomed with Marlowe, was arrested and questioned— actually tortured. Kyd died shortly after his release. The investigators required Marlowe to report to them daily. Fanaticism flung out its dragnet, and soon after Marlowe was slain. There was a general feeling throughout London that he had met a deserved death.

The author of *A Groats-worth*, whether Greene or Chettle, expressed bitter prejudice and made what was intended to be a devastating attack:

> Base-minded men, all three of you [presumably Peele and Nash and one other dramatist], if by my misery ye be not warned; for unto none of you (like me) sought those burs to cleave; those puppets, I mean, that speak from our mouths, those antics garnished in our colours. . . . It is a pity men of . . . rare wits should be subject to the pleasures of such rude grooms. . . . There is an upstart Crow, beautified with our feathers, that with his Tygers hart wrapt in a Player's hyde, supposes he is as well able to bombast out a blanke verse as the best of you; and being an absolute *Johannes fac totum*, is in his own conceit the onely Shake-scene in a countrey.

Some have thought "Shake-scene" referred to the tragedian Edward Alleyn, though Chettle definitely tells us that "Shake-scene" was a playwright. That he was Shakespeare has been generally accepted, and for that reason this notorious vomiting of spleen has held attention out of proportion to its significance. If, as seems practically certain, it was an attack on Shakespeare, it is of less importance than some have supposed, since aside from hurting his feelings it did Shakespeare no injury. To the contrary, by making him appear a victim of jealousy, it brought him favorable publicity.

From the term *Johannes fac totum* it is clear that "Shake-scene" had been turning his hand in more than one direction. The "do-all" meaning of the Latin term compels some interpretation: either he was an actor who was trying to win acclaim also as a playwright; or he had had more than one play on the stage; or he had written plays of all types—comedy, tragedy, and chronicle history.

Genius is aware of its own ability. From the accusation that "Shake-scene" overvalued himself, we may well believe that Shakespeare had displayed considerable ego. A man who does that tends to chill affection. We should not assume that when Shakespeare began to write for the London theaters he was a perfectly lovable character and that his self-sufficiency did not irritate and exasperate envious rivals. Though an idealized image of the bard might be more pleasant, we must cling to an image that is credible. Surely Shakespeare could not have achieved the stature of the author of these great plays if he had not from the outset carried the firm conviction that he would become the supreme shaker of scenes.

The attacks in *A Groats-worth* went beyond gentlemanly bounds. They were personal affronts. The accusation against Marlowe was close to being a death warrant. Shakespeare, though not materially injured, had been insulted. Feeling that he had been one of the persons slurred at by the terms "burs," "puppets," "antics," and "grooms," he was deeply aggrieved. Chettle knew how the attacks had hurt both Marlowe and Shakespeare. Because he had been the editor (and perhaps the author?) of *A Groats-worth*, Chettle voluntarily assumed sole responsibility for it and sought to make amends. In his *Epistle to Kind-Hearts Dream*, published in December 1592, Chettle said: "I am sorry, as if the original fault had been my fault." He felt that he owed both Marlowe and "Shake-scene" an apology,

107

but with a difference. The stench of atheism was to be shunned like the plague, and in Marlowe's case the accusation was so patently well founded that Chettle had reason to fear that he might himself get burned with hell's fire if he should even meet the sulphurous dramatist. And so Chettle wrote: "With neither of them that take offence was I acquainted, and with one of them I care not if I never be."

In the case of "Shake-scene," however, in order to counter the public effect of the unfairness, Chettle met the young playwright and published his impression of him as a man. Chettle found "his demeanor no less civil than he excellent in the quality he professes. Besides, divers of worship have reported his uprightness of dealing, which argues his honesty, and his facetious grace in writing, that approves his Art." Thus Chettle found the writer's character commendable, and he saw in him a man of an original mind who was not a borrower or plagiarist, as *A Groats-worth* had charged, but a writer who was giving far more than he was taking.

Two of Shakespeare's sonnets clearly echo the emotional experience caused by *A Groats-worth*. Sonnet 111 tells us that in connection with his chosen profession his "name receives a brand." So apt a pun as "Shake-scene" must have stuck to the playwright—an unforgettable nickname. Shakespeare no doubt heard that byword of derision so often from the lips of acquaintances and even from strangers in the streets, that he felt he had indeed been branded with it:

> O, for my sake do you with Fortune chide,
> The guilty goddess of my harmful deeds,
> That did not better for my life provide
> Than public means which public manners breeds.
> Thence comes it that my name receives a brand,
> And almost thence my nature is subdued
> To what it works in, like the dyer's hand.
>
> [Sonnet 111]

In Sonnet 112 Shakespeare says his friend's love for him compensates for "vulgar scandal stamp'd upon my brow"—what in the preceding sonnet he had called a "brand." The poet will "strive" to give ear only to "shames and praises" expressed by the friend, and make himself impervious to "others' voices." In this Sonnet 112 there is an unmistakable pun on Greene. With it, the poet's reactions patently are those stirred by the attack publicly believed to have been by Greene. The "critic" presumably had been Nash or Greene, and the "flatterer" was very likely Chettle.

> Your love and pity doth the impression fill
> Which vulgar scandal stamp'd upon my brow;
> For what care I who calls me well or ill,
> So you o'er-green my bad, my good allow?
> You are my all the world, and I must strive
> To know my shames and praises from your tongue; . . .
> In so profound abysm I throw all care
> Of others' voices, that my adder's sense
> To critic and to flatterer stopped are.
>
> [Sonnet 112]

14

THE PLANTED NAME

"Your name from hence immortal life shall have."

SONNET 81

*T*HE DEDICATION PAGE OF THE *Sonnets* VOLUME IN 1609 was not by Shakespeare but by the printer. Many have assumed from this that the printer was publishing the sonnets without the poet's participation or permission. Ivor Brown says: "It is possible that Thorpe got hold of them by backstairs methods."[1] Several considerations, however, argue the contrary.

Sir Edmund Chambers says: "It does not seem to me likely, in view of the character of the sonnets in the second series, that the whole collection can have been kept together by anyone but Shakespeare himself. And if so, it is most likely that the arrangement of 1609 was his."[2]

No one has presented a better arrangement. Hilton Landry says: "Sonnets which fall together belong together," and "Connected sonnets are in the proper sequence since nearly always each sonnet grows out of its predecessor."[3] If the arrangement of the printed *Sonnets* was Shakespeare's, then the volume was in all probability printed with his cooperation.

Strong evidence that Shakespeare cooperated in the publication lies in the fact that the *Sonnets* were given to the public in the spring of 1609. Why then? We need not be partial to intricate explanations when there is before us one that is simple and natural. It is based upon our having seen a compelling reason why Shakespeare had the highest respect for his father's character, and presumably also for his mother's character and her good opinion of himself.

In biographical studies one is often led to a discovery by the closeness of two dates. In the present case, close dates suggest a relationship between something that happened in the poet's family and the publication of the *Sonnets*. Shakespeare's father had been dead for several years, but his mother did not die until September of 1608. The *Sonnets* were entered for publication on May 20, 1609. Had Shakespeare previously been deterred from publishing his sonnets because the subject matter in many of them would have deeply shocked his parents? Did his mother's death open the way for their publication?* His wife was living, but there is much in the sonnets to warrant the guess that he had either come to an understanding with her in regard to his sex life away from home, or was defiant of, or indifferent to, her reaction.

Further, the 1609 volume contains strong internal evidence that it was published with the poet's full cooperation. No one, it seems, has hitherto observed all the implications of the dedicatory page:

TO. THE. ONLIE. BEGETTER. OF.
THESE. INSUING. SONNETS.
MR. W. H. ALL. HAPPINESSE.
AND. THAT. ETERNITIE.
PROMISED.
BY.
OUR. EVER-LIVING. POET.
WISHETH.

* "When Shakespeare's mother died we should infer that he was actually overwhelmed for it cannot have been only the affairs of estate settlement that kept him away from London for such a long period that sad autumn when he lingered in Stratford until long after the theatrical season had commenced.... And in the year following we find him writing *Coriolanus* with the leading female character a mother."[4]

THE. WELL-WISHING.
ADVENTURER. IN.
SETTING.
FORTH.
T.T.

Since the dedication is by the printer, T. T. (Thomas Thorpe), it is valid to ask: Why was the dedication not by Shakespeare himself?

The reason appears with clarity after we observe the force of "that eternitie promised by our ever-living poet." This eternity was the immortality Shakespeare promises to his young friend in Sonnets 17, 18, and 19, and in the following lines from eight other sonnets:

> Not marble, nor the gilded monuments
> Of princes, shall outlive this powerful rhyme;
> ... Your praise shall still find room
> Even in the eyes of all posterity.
>
> [Sonnet 55]

> And yet to times in hope my verse shall stand,
> Praising thy worth.
>
> [Sonnet 60]

> His beauty shall in these black lines seen,
> And they shall live, and he in them still green.
>
> [Sonnet 63]

> ... in black ink my love shall still shine bright.
>
> [Sonnet 65]

> Your name from hence immortal life shall have, ...
> Your monument shall be my gentle verse,
> Which eyes not yet created shall o'er-read;
> And tongues to be, your being shall rehearse,
> When all the breathers of this world are dead;
> You still shall live—such virtue hath my pen—
> Where breath most breathes, even in the mouths of men.
>
> [Sonnet 81]

113

Muse . . . 't lies in thee
To make him much outlive a gilded tomb
And to be praised of ages yet to be.

[Sonnet 101]

I'll live in this poor rhyme, . . .
And thou in this shalt find thy monument,
When tyrants' crests and tombs of brass are spent.

[Sonnet 107]

It seems irrational to believe that the man to whom the printer wished eternity was any other than the man who had inspired the poet's repeated promises of eternity. The immortality so lavishly promised could not with any aptness be applied to a man who had merely collected for the printer manuscripts which had been in the hands of various persons. Linguistic usage favors "inspirer" and not "procurer" as the meaning of "begetter." [5] The reasonable conclusion is that "W. H." were the initials of Shakespeare's friend. Also, the promised immortality had not yet materialized, and we shall see how the dedicatory page was devised by the poet, though ostensibly by the printer, to help make that materialization certain.

Why Shakespeare did not himself sign the dedicatory page for the *Sonnets* volume should now be obvious. He did not sign that page because most of the sonnets, at least five-sixths of them, were in themselves dedications to the young man who had inspired them. If the poet had himself presented a formal dedication, it would have been redundant. Worse than that, it would have been in questionable taste. Some of the sonnets were uncomplimentary to the friend, and herein we see an additional reason why the poet refrained from assuming responsibility for "dedicated words which writers use of their fair subject, blessing every book" (Sonnet 82). A general dedication would have appeared to praise some things which had caused him jealousy and great unhappiness. Being a sensitive person, Shakespeare simply could not have signed a general dedication. He properly left that to the printer.

The case of the *Sonnets* is quite different from that of Shakespeare's plays printed during his lifetime in pirated editions. From the point of view of a printer, the *Sonnets* volume was not in the same
114   hopeful category with plays whose popularity on the stage guaran-

teed rewarding sales for printed versions, no matter how garbled. In its dedication the printer Thorpe realistically calls himself "the adventurer." He was indeed risking his money on the *Sonnets*. He was praying that their sale would be large enough to reimburse him for the cost of printing. Thorpe was aware that he was adventuring against a probable loss. As a business venture the *Sonnets* volume was not so promising as *Venus and Adonis* and *The Rape of Lucrece*, whose sexy titles and the fact that they were sensational stories were factors favorable to their success. Something special had to be put into the *Sonnets* volume to catch the attention of prospective buyers.

We know what that special something was. It was placed on the dedicatory page. If anyone knew the value of publicity, it was Shakespeare as a playwright. He had a practical reason for revealing the initials of his friend at the time of the first publication. He knew that a dedication to an unknown "Mr. W. H." whose identity had not yet been unearthed, would arouse curiosity and reader interest. He was perceptive enough to foresee that it would start tongues wagging as they have wagged ever since. The printing of "Mr. W. H." evinced someone's knowledge of the identity. But the secret was kept by giving only initials. The printer's use of them is practically conclusive evidence that they had been furnished by the poet, the only person who could assure him of their correctness.

Max Meredith Reese says: "Although there is no record of it, the publication of the Sonnets possibly led to a protest and the withdrawal of the issue. . . . The Sonnets had to wait until 1640 for a second printing. It is possible that Thorpe found himself in trouble, perhaps from Shakespeare, perhaps from Mr. W. H." [6] But the words Reese here uses: "no record . . . possibly . . . possible . . . perhaps . . . perhaps" are a fivefold indulgence in groundless surmise. The words "had to wait until 1640 for a second printing" are, however, factual. The printer had ventured against the chances of poor sales.

At first, while writing the sonnets to his friend, Shakespeare had wanted to remain anonymous: "My name be buried" (Sonnets 71, 72). But we know from Meres that by the year 1598 he had changed his mind and had begun letting some sonnets circulate among his friends. "I may not evermore acknowledge thee" (Sonnet 36) expresses his feeling that his friend's name is the one that should not be divulged. So also:

In my tongue
Thy sweet beloved name no more shall dwell,
Lest I, too much profane, should do it wrong,
And haply of our old acquaintance tell.

[Sonnet 89]

After saying in some of the sonnets at the time he wrote them that no one must know the identity of the friend, was there any reason why the poet might have revealed the friend's initials in 1609? Yes. A long time—more than fifteen years—had gone by since the writing of the bulk of the sonnets. The friend was not someone Shakespeare had first met in London, whose name the initials would immediately reveal to many Londoners. He was a friend or "old acquaintance" from another part of the country, with their early association now obscured by both time and distance. No one could know with certainty the friend's name merely from the initials. At the same time there is evidence to justify belief that Shakespeare revealed the initials deliberately because he wanted them to serve as a clue to ultimate discovery of the identity— discovery after he and the friend were both dead. It may be argued from Sonnet 81: "Tongues to be your being shall rehearse When all the breathers of this world are dead," that the poet expected that his friend's name would in some distant future day be made public.

Let us not be so intrigued by the initials as to ignore the meaning of "Mr." in Shakespeare's day. In the absence of any suggestion that the friend was a ship's captain, a schoolmaster, a scholar of approved erudition, an artist of distinguished skill, or a legal functionary, the "Mr." (meaning "Master"), as used in 1609, tells us that "Mr. W. H." was not of the titled nobility. He was not an earl, for example. The heir apparent to a Scottish peerage below the rank of earl could be addressed as "Master," but one in the rank of earl could not be. The "Mr." also indicates that "W. H." was not of as high a rank as knight. Down to the early sixteenth century, "Master" could legally be prefixed to the name of a knight or bishop, but not later. Avoiding conflict with these considerations, A. L. Rowse advances a theory that the beloved youth in the *Sonnets* was the Earl of Southampton, and that "Mr. W. H." was not Shakespeare's friend, but was the man who collected the sonnets for the printer. Rowse says: "The Countess of Southampton . . . usually referred to her second and third husbands, Sir Thomas Heneage and Sir William Harvey, as Master Heneage and Master Harvey. It was regular form." [7] Indeed, it was regular form and customary for a wife in speaking to a third person to call her husband "Master," just as a husband called his wife "Mistress." But a public use of "Master" in a printed dedication was a very different thing from its social use in marital reference.

Rowse's theory fails to fit the findings of chronological order and dating. A most serious objection to it is that belief in it vitiates the power of the sonnets by removing from them any deep spiritual significance. Rowse calls the sonnets to the friend "duty pieces." He says: "The Sonnets are throughout from first to last duty-sonnets." [8] This assertion is severely handled by John Leslie Hotson who says: "Ordinary common sense dismisses the Just So Story which informs the credulous reader that 'Shakespeare was hired by a worried mother to write a lot of poems to make her son marry.' Only complete bafflement could force even a theorist unacquainted with the Elizabethans to suggest such an absurdity." [9]

In 1579 the *Shepherd's Calendar* was dedicated to "Maister Philip Sidney," and Stephen Gosson's *The Schoole of Abuse* was dedicated to "the right noble Gentleman, Master Philip Sidney, Esquier," both of them before Master Sidney was knighted. The carelessness with which recent writers have stated that these publications in 1579 were dedicated to "Sir Philip Sidney" shows the general ignorance today of what were correct prefixes to names in Elizabethan times. The proper form for dedicating a literary work to a knight was "To the Right Worshipfull," as we see from John Northbrook's *A Treatise wherein Dicing, Dauncing, Vaine Playes . . . are reproved*. If "Mr. W. H." were the eldest son of a peer or of a knight, he could not have been called "Esquier." So far as we have record, Shakespeare was himself first called "Mr." after the Shakespeare coat of arms was granted and he thus became enrolled as a member of a family of the gentry.

In so far as it was indicative of social rank or degree, "Master" in the early seventeenth century was prefixed to the name of a man below the rank of a knight and above the common level. There is no reason to assume that the "Mr." in the printer's dedication of Shakespeare's *Sonnets* was anything but a scrupulously legal ascription which neither belittled nor unduly exalted the social status of "W. H." It seems practically certain that "Mr. W. H." was a Gentleman, a member of the class called the gentry. If he were a knight or of higher rank than a knight, the printer would have been putting himself in danger of the law by calling him "Mr." It was a punishable offense to attach to a name a prefix or suffix that gave the bearer a lower rank than the one to which he was legally entitled. Nor could one with impunity attach a prefix or suffix that gave the bearer a higher rank than he actually had. Even to recent times these have been punishable offenses under British law. As late as the eighteen-nineties a man was haled into court under that law and fined £5 for having accepted from the Post Office letters improperly addressed to him as "Esquire." While such a law is no longer operative, it illustrates the seriousness with which proper name usages were regarded in Shakespeare's day.

When Sonnets 1 to 17 were composed, some years after the writing of the main body of the sequence, "Mr. W. H." had at some time in the interval reached marriageable age. What in those days was a marriageable age? Thought of in terms of sex, marriage was considered by some people desirable at puberty. Marriages like Shakespeare's at eighteen or even younger were not uncommon. However, Shakespeare began urging his friend to marry only several years after he might well have married, and it was this unduly extended bachelorhood which provided a natural opening for the urging.

At this point some readers no doubt hope a magician will put his hand into the hat and draw out the rabbit. Who actually was "Mr. W. H."?

Some people decry any prying into a poet's private life. They feel it presumptuous and objectionable, or beneath a scholar's dignity. Lewis says: "The literary historian . . . would not give a farthing to know the identity of the 'man right fair.' "[10]

Can there be any justification for pursuing inquiry in this matter? Is the identification of "Mr. W. H." of any importance aside from satisfying curiosity? Yes, most decidedly. We know with certainty from several sonnets that Shakespeare expected that the name would some day be unearthed, and keenly wanted it to be. Also, an acceptable theory as to the identity—that is, a theory that fits all the requirements—might lead to discovery of evidence that would conclusively prove it correct. In that case the facts of time and place and the attendant circumstances of Shakespeare's first meeting with his friend would be of prime biographical importance, opening further vistas into the poet's formative years. Furthermore—though this is wishful thinking—a correct identification which would inevitably stimulate a search in old attics in the region where "Mr. W. H." resided, might result in the rewarding discovery of yellowed papers, among them sonnets to the friend in Shakespeare's handwriting.

The above use of the phrase "an acceptable theory" is equivalent to saying that no theory hitherto brought forward fits all the requirements as we now know them to be. Let us see whether we have at last a theory that does fit them all.

The findings in Appendix B, applied to those findings in Chapter Two, point to 1589 as the year when Shakespeare began writing sonnets to the friend. In light of this dating, two statements by Keen and Lubbock take on significance. These writers have said that in 1588, "Shakespeare may have been with the Queen's Players at New Park, October 10, this year," and in 1589, "Shakespeare may have been at Knowsley in June." My attention was thereby drawn to Lancashire. Was it in Lancashire that Shakespeare met "Mr. W. H."?

Repetitious punning on the name "Will" in Sonnets 135, 136, and 143 has been widely accepted as indicating that the friend's first name was also William. I examined the Lancashire records, looking for a young man among the families of the gentry in Lancashire with whom Shakespeare presumably had been acquainted in his pre-London years. It had to be a youth whose initials were "W. H.," whose first name was William, whose social status was "Mr.," and whom Shakespeare might have seen, or observed the beauty of, for the first time in 1589; further, one whose age would fit perfectly with Shakespeare's having written the main body of the sonnets to the friend in 1589–93, and the Sonnets 1 to 17, urging the friend to marry, a few years thereafter. In the Lancashire parish records there was one young man and only one who qualified in all particulars. When Professor Louis Marder, editor of *Shakespeare Newsletter*, heard that I had found such a likely candidate, he urgently requested me to let him publish my theory as to the identity of Shakespeare's friend. I gave permission, and in a communication stated why I believed that "Mr.

119

W. H." was the Lancashire youth, Mr. William Houghton. This first publication of the William Houghton theory was in 1958.[11]

The conviction grew in my mind that Shakespeare wanted readers of the *Sonnets* to accept more than the mere fact that such a beautiful youth had once existed. The poet's repeated expressions of certainty that his friend's name would live in the future on men's lips, were definite intimations that the poet had planted the name in at least one of his sonnets. But in which sonnet? John Leslie Hotson was surely right in saying in 1964: "Somewhere in these poems it must be lying in full view, unseen."[12]

In a paper read before the Andiron Club of New York City, Dr. Stanley Rypins of Brooklyn College had said that when a poet planted a name, he customarily left the word "name" as a clue to what he had concealed. There are two instances of this in Edgar Allan Poe: the three names of a girl buried in his "An Enigma," and the name of another girl in his poem "A Valentine."

Was the word "name" in Shakespeare's sonnets a clue to name planting? In Sonnet 81 Shakespeare used the word "name" in a context that seemed suspiciously like a definite assertion that he had planted the last name of "Mr. W. H.":

> Your name from hence immortal life shall have.

In reference to this specific language in Sonnet 81, Hotson said: "Here he is unmistakable. For how could he possibly give that name immortality *by these sonnets unless he put that name into them?* It must be there." The italics are Hotson's.[13]

Hotson pointed to the right place to find the planted name. However, in his pursuit of a theory, he looked for it in many other places. His theory was that "Mr. W. H." was William Hatclyffe of Lincolnshire, whose extant signatures are spelled "Hatclyffe." Hotson could not, however, find "cliff" in any sonnet. (Surely Shakespeare had ingenuity enough to incorporate "cliff" into at least one sonnet.) Hotson was undeterred. Determined to substantiate his theory, he found "hat" in "what" and in "that," and he found "life" and "live" in the same sonnets with "what" and "that." From these he constructed "hatlife" and "hatlive" and asked his readers to accept these as variants of "Hatclyffe." He cited forty occurrences of "what" and "that" in the same sonnets

as "live" or "life." He also seized upon "leave." He found these
in thirty-five sonnets, and thought to triumph over the inadequacy
of his demonstration by saying: "What rules out accident here is
the overwhelming mass of occurrences." What Hotson failed to rule
out is the frequent occurrence in the English language of the words
"what," "that," "life," and "live."

But the line, "Your name from hence immortal life shall
have," to which Hotson had pointed with instinctive insight,
though with unseeing eyes, is so significant that it demands close
attention to the entire Sonnet 81:

> Or I shall live your epitaph to make,
> Or you survive when I in earth am rotten;
> From hence your memory death cannot take,
> Although in me each part will be forgotten.
> Your name from hence immortal life shall have,
> Though I, once gone, to all the world must die!
> The earth can yield me but a common grave,
> When you entombed in men's eyes shall lie.
> Your monument shall be my gentle verse,
> Which eyes not yet created shall o'er-read;
> And tongues to be your being shall rehearse,
> When all the breathers of this world are dead;
> > You still shall live—such virtue hath my pen—
> > Where breath most breathes, even in the mouths of men.

If the poet planted the beloved name anywhere in his sonnets,
he must have planted it in this one. In telling us that we may
find in his verse "each part" of the name, he hints that he has
given the name in separate syllables. It was not until 1965, seven
years after I had published my belief that Mr. William Houghton
was the young man, and only after Hotson had pointed to Sonnet
81, that I first saw that the name Houghton was planted in it in
association with the clue line. Three years later, my friend Arthur
Godfrey of Pictou asked me to look further into Sonnet 81. He wrote
me that there is another clue line: "From hence your memory
death cannot take"; that by the repetition of the phrase "from
hence" the poet was doubling his assurance that the name would
someday be detected; that the word "rehearse" which in
Shakespeare's day meant "repeat," is a hint that the name has

121

been planted twice in the sonnet; that the logical position for each planting is in association with each "from hence." Thus prompted, I observed that the name Houghton is planted twice in Sonnet 81, and then I further observed that in the line, "When you entombed in men's eyes shall lie," the poet hints that the reader should look for the name as spelled, as seen "in men's eyes"; and in the words "in the mouths of men" the poet hints that the reader should look for the name as pronounced.

It is precisely thus that we find the name twice in Sonnet 81, in one instance with one letter off from the proper spelling, but given as pronounced, and in the other, correctly spelled.

This is not all. When Professor Irving Linn, a specialist in the evolution of the English language, informed me that in Elizabethan times "how" was pronounced "hoe," there came inevitably the discovery that also in the adjacent Sonnet 80 the poet had planted the name:

> O! how I faint when I of you do write,
> Knowing a better spirit doth use your name,
> And in the praise thereof spends all his might,
> To make me tongue-tied, speaking of your fame!
>
> [Sonnet 80]

The word "speaking" is a hint that the name has been planted in this sonnet not as spelled, but as pronounced.

In another sonnet we are given hints that the name has been planted in it: "thy budding name," "tongue that tells," and "naming thy name," and these phrases tell us that the name has been planted as pronounced.

> How sweet and lovely dost thou make the shame
> Which, like a canker in the fragrant rose,
> Doth spot the beauty of thy budding name!
> O, in what sweets dost thou thy sins inclose!
> That tongue that tells the story of thy days,
> Making lascivious comments on thy sport,
> Cannot dispraise but in a kind of praise;
> Naming thy name blesses an ill report!
>
> [Sonnet 95]

Shakespeare planted the name "Houghton" four times, not just anywhere, but in three sonnets in each of which he gave unmistakable clues to his having done so, and he planted the name only where he had given such clues.

While there were Houghtons in other shires, Shakespeare's planting of the name Houghton takes force as a Lancashire evidence, in view of Alexander Houghton's Will, and because of the evidences which, seven years before I discovered the planting, caused the shaping of the theory that "Mr. W. H." was Mr. William Houghton of Lancashire.

And so we find buried in each of three sonnets in proximity to the word "name" the two syllables of the last name of "Mr. W. H.":

IN SONNET 80:

line 1. O! HOW I faint when I of you do write

line 4. To make me TONgue-tied, speaking of your fame

IN SONNET 81:

line 4 AltHOUGH in me each part will be forgotTEN

line 6. T HOUGH I, once gone, to all the world must die

line 11. And TONgues to be your being shall rehearse

IN SONNET 95:

line 1. HOW sweet and lovely dost thou make the shame

line 4. That TONgue that tells the story of thy days

Observe the logical positioning of all the name plantings:

	First syllable of name	*Second syllable of name*
In Sonnet 80	First accented syllable of a line	Second accented syllable of a later line
In Sonnet 81:	First word of line 4	Last word of line 4
	First syllable of line 6	Second syllable of line 11
In Sonnet 95:	First word of first quatrain	Second word of second quatrain

123

The occurrence of the name in these logical positions is surely by more than mere chance. Such skillful positioning must have been the handiwork of the poet, and with extraordinary cleverness. It seems fair to say that by Shakespeare's own testimony, "Mr. W. H." was Mr. William Houghton, and that the name William Houghton will have what the poet promised—immortal life. Art is linked not with the ephemeral but the eternal. To note the time is to strip away time, and reveal what has survived. This belated uncovering of the name to which the poet promised immortality confirms the poet's faith that the beloved name would outlive monuments of brass.

Mr. William Houghton (pronounced "Hoe-ton"), was a nephew of the Alexander Houghton who left a legacy to William Shakeshafte. He was the second son of Alexander Houghton's half-brother Thomas of Lea and of Hoghton Tower. His father, Thomas, was at one time Sheriff of Lancashire, and became auditor to the Earl of Derby. Thomas Houghton was killed in a feudistic battle at Lea, November 21, 1589. "Dear my love," Shakespeare wrote in Sonnet 13, "you know you had a father."

William Houghton's mother was Ann Kighley, daughter of Sir John Kighley. William's elder brother, Richard, was born August 26, 1570. Richard "succeeded to a very great estate, was knighted by Queen Elizabeth, and was made a baronet with the first advanced to the dignity."[14] He became Sheriff of Lancashire in 1599, and several times represented Lancashire in Parliament.

Mr. William Houghton was the second of seventeen children born to his parents in nineteen years. He was therefore almost certainly born in 1571, or within a few months thereafter. He was seventeen or eighteen when Shakespeare was first attracted to "Mr. W. H."

As a member of one of the wealthy families of Lancashire, whose political activities took them to Parliament, William Houghton had the means and the opportunity to visit London if he so desired.*

---

* The principal Lancashire families were well acquainted with each other and did much visiting in each others' houses as we see from an entry in December 1587 in the Stanley Papers: "On Saturday Sr Thos. Hesketh, Players wente awaie, and the same day Dr. Edward Halsoll, Mr. Houghton of Houghton and many strandgers came to Knowsley. On Sunday Mr. Houghton departed and Sr Ryc. Shirborne came...." The same records show that entertaining in the Lancashire manor houses began each year in June, and reached a climax at Christmas.

Did Shakespeare's urging his friend to marry have any effect? When did William Houghton marry? Since his elder brother married in 1590 at the age of twenty, William Houghton's marriage was presumably after that. Both he and his widowed mother married into the same family. His mother Ann, who gave birth to her firstborn in 1570 and was widowed in 1589, then became the third wife of Sir Richard Sherburne (1546–1629) of Stoneyhurst, after his second wife, Catherine, a niece of the Earl of Derby, died in 1591.

Mr. William Houghton married a half sister of Sir Richard Sherburne. His wife was Grace Sherburne, daughter of another Sir Richard Sherburne (1526–1594) of Stoneyhurst. This Sir Richard was one of the most conspicuous figures in the history of Lancashire. He was several times in Parliament.

Mr. William Houghton* resided in Grimsargh, six miles north-east of Lea. There he and his wife Grace had six children: William, Richard, Thomas, Catherine, Isabel, and Ann. Grace was living in Grimsargh Hall in 1638–39. Mr. William Houghton died in 1642. Since he lived to the age of seventy, it would seem that he was a person above average in physical vitality.

---

* A playwright with a name of a different spelling, William Haughton, collaborated with Henry Chettle Thomas Dekker, John Day, and Richard Hathway. William Haughton was working for the Admiral's Company from 1597, in which year he was referred to as "yonge." Anyone who wishes to think that William Haughton, playwright in London, and Mr. William Houghton of Grimsargh in Lancashire, might have been the same person, should note that Shakespeare in Sonnet 82 says: "I grant thou wert not married to my Muse."

15

SHAKESPEARE'S FACE

" 'Tis my picture;
Refuse it not."

TWELFTH NIGHT, 3.4.203–204

W HAT DID SHAKESPEARE LOOK LIKE IN HIS MATURITY?
Did he resemble the bust in Stratford Church? Or
did he resemble the engraving by Droeshout in the First Folio?
One would hope neither. But until recently it seemed improbable
that it could ever be convincingly demonstrated that we have a
portrait of the mature poet painted from life. Now, however, it
seems practically certain that we have such a portrait.

When King James VI of Scotland became King James I of
England, he naturally had no desire to perpetuate the memory of
Queen Elizabeth, who had ordered his mother's execution. He made
as clean a sweep as he could of all associations with her. One of his
first acts, less than a month after he became King of England, was
to change the name of the Chamberlain's Men to King's Players.
He far outdid Queen Elizabeth as patron of the arts, and whereas, 127

during the last ten years under Queen Elizabeth, Shakespeare's Company had performed at Court on an average of less than four times a year, during the first nine years under King James it gave on an average fourteen Court performances a year. Also, whereas the parsimonious Queen had paid £10 for a Court performance, King James paid £30.

Scarlet, a symbol of blood and hence of power, was the royal color of Scotland, and King James ordered his Master of the Wardrobe to issue to each of the King's Players 4½ yards of red cloth, costing ten shillings per yard, for a costume to be worn in his Coronation Procession. The list of recipients of the cloth in order named was "Wm. Shakespeare, A. Phillips, L. Fletcher, J. Hemminge, R.B.,* W. Sly, Robt. Armin, H. Condell, Rich. Cowley."[1]

Preparations for the Procession included seven arches of triumph, construction of which began in April and went on until Bartholomew-tide, and then ceased temporarily because of mortality from the plague. King James was crowned privately. The Coronation Parade was postponed until March 15 of the following year—1604.

That day, "King James . . . made his Royall Passage through the Citie. . . . Five Triumphs were paid for by Citizens and the Chamber of London. Two arches erected by Merchant Strangers, were their own particular charge."[2] Sixteen committees had worked on these five archways, and one hundred and forty carpenters under Stephen Harrison, who hired seven master painters to decorate them. Ben Jonson made a design for the first arch at Fenchurch Street, crowded with figures and Latin quotations. The second gate, in Grasse-Street (later Gracious, now Gracechurch), was erected and elaborately decorated by the Italians. The third gate on Cornhill by the Exchange, representing the seventeen Provinces of Belgia, or the Dutch nation, and by them raised, touched the house fronts on both sides. It was over eighty feet in height, had a large central arch through which the King would ride, and side arches for pedestrians. The Dutch merchants resident in London, determined not to be outdone by the Italians, had Dutch and Flemish artists cover their gate completely with magnificent murals on both sides.[3]

* Everyone knew the initials of the leading actor, Richard Burbage, just as we know G.B.S.

128

The order of paraders in the Coronation Procession was: Messengers of the Chamber and Harbingers, Porters, Gentlemen and Esquires, Servants of the Princes and King and Queen, Clerks of the Seal and the Council, Parliament and the Council, Chaplains, Aldermen, the Prince's Council, the Queen's Council, the King's Advocate, Sir Francis Bacon, Sergeants at Law, Masters of Chancellery, Secretaries of the Latin and French tongues, Sewers, Carvers, Cup Bearers; the Masters of the Tents, Revels (including Shakespeare and the other King's Players, probably on horseback so that they could be better seen by the spectators), the Masters of the Armoury, Ordnance; Barons of the Exchequer, Judges of Law, the Chief Justices, Knights, Earls, etc., Nobles, the King.

In the months of 1603–1604 during which the plague compelled the closing of the theaters, Shakespeare had an unanticipated period of leisure. It was then he and Ben Jonson had their portrait painted by Karel van Mander, one of the artists from the Netherlands who had come to London. Karel van Mander (1548–1606) was born in Meulebeecke near Courtrai. He studied for four years in Italy, and returned to found a Painting Academy in Haarlem. He was the teacher of Frans Hals. He was away from home "traveling" in 1603, and in 1604 went to Amsterdam, where he became the Principal of an Academy for Poetry. His *Schilderboeck* (Painter Book), most of it written in 1603, was published in Amsterdam in 1604.

In view of the importance ascribed to the Coronation display, and the prominence of van Mander among artists in the Netherlands, and considering also that he had previously assisted in making a richly decorated triumphal arch in Vienna for the reception of the Emperor Rudolph, it seems practically certain that he participated in preparing the Dutch gate in London.* As

---

* Strong evidence points to van Mander's having contributed to the decorative and allegorical paintings on the Dutch gate. John Nichols thus describes some of its "adornments many": In addition to scenes of "husbandrie" and "men weaving, women spinning, the children at their hand-loomes" and a market scene with a "Frau and Burgher buying and selling," there was "a large table [board or canvas], in which is their fishing and shipping lively and sweetely set down." There were also allegories of Time, Truth, Art, Sedulity, Labour. Among the works of van Mander is a market scene with a soldier and marketwoman buying and selling (Plate 124 in Paatz), a "Fischenstechen von einem Schiff aus," and an "Allegorie auf die Wahrheit." Several interests drew van Mander to London. He had an

129

a teacher of art he would have felt it incumbent upon him to see the triumphal arches in London.

Passages in van Mander's *Schilderboeck* show that its author knew London well. He lists England as one of the countries his art students should visit, and he states that he has himself traveled far and wide in pursuing acquaintance with works of art. "I have visited many cities." The implication is unavoidable that he had visited the cities which contain the paintings he describes. He speaks of pictures by Holbein and others which could be seen in England, and he tells in what collections they can be found: Whitehall, Chirugijnshal (Surgeons Hall), Jacob I (King James I), Howard, Pembroke. As one who has seen pictures by Holbein in England, he says the portrait of the king is life-size.

> In various houses there are still so many and beautiful paintings by Holbein that it is amazing how he was able to produce all these marvelous works during his lifetime. . . . At London, in the banquet hall of the Hanseatic League there are two splendid watercolors on canvas. . . . One of the best by Holbein is at present in the house of a member of the nobility, a certain Mr. Coop,* who is a lover of art, living outside of London, at Temple Bar, across from the Lord Treasurer, who has in his house many other beautiful paintings by Holbein and works of other artists.[4]

The first part of van Mander's *Schilderboeck* was a "Didactic Poem," the first published material by a Netherlander on the theory and practice of painting. The second part consisted of biographies of painters and is our chief source of information regarding Flemish painters, of the fourteenth and fifteenth centuries, and of several Italian painters not dealt with by Vasari.

---

uncle, François van Mander, who was buried there, and for whom he painted an epitaph. Himself a dramatist, he was interested in the London theaters, and he shared this interest with one of his friends in Holland who visited him in 1602–1603, eloquently praised his *Schilderboeck* and commissioned him to paint two pictures in Amsterdam. This friend was Canon de Witt, the man who gave us a sketch of the Swan Theatre.

Coop is a misprint for Coke, Sir Edward Coke, knighted May 22, 1603, in which month he was both "Mr." and " a member of the nobility " as van Mander calls him. His house was north of Temple Bar across Lincoln's Inn Fields from the Lord Treasurer's. Coke possessed Holbein's portraits of Sir Thomas More, of Fox, Bishop of Winchester, and of Fisher, Bishop of Rochester.

A broadly cultivated man of the late Renaissance, van Mander was interested in the accomplishments of other men in poetry, drama, and painting. In addition to religious pictures, landscapes, and portraits, he made engravings of secular subjects: St. Bartholomew's Massacre, depicting Admiral Coligny being thrown from a window; a peasant wedding, two pictures of Haarlem, and many allegories, among them one called "The Discussions of the Poets." He handled his subjects in a free and individual way, and was "a jester, merry and witty," a man after Shakespeare's own heart.

Van Mander's "Didactic Poem" enunciated his theories of portraiture. This instructive work by the artist who was the teacher of Frans Hals has not been published in English, more's the pity, and the passages quoted are translated from a German edition. Van Mander said:

> In your drawing, show persons in movement like cultivated actors. ... Express emotions through gestures, but not theatrical ones. ... A good accomplishment will be found in your human figures which at rest appear alive. Take care to build them on the foundation of the poets. ... When you go to inventing, be acutely attentive and make yourself thoroughly acquainted with the subject [theme, substance] of your project through repeated reading; for it will not hurt if you have impressed in memory the correct circumstances of the story you design to tell. ... In a painting go earnestly about it to build the sense of a story. In everything they undertake, painters have the same privileges as the poets. In a picture include divers objects which are allegorically significant of the characteristic qualities of the persons.[5]

There are some today who deny that "painters have the same privileges as the poets" of building "the sense of a story." It seems likely that as a narrative and dramatic poet Shakespeare would have heartily subscribed to van Mander's theory.

Believing in thorough preparation to create a picture, van Mander studied his subjects, in this case Shakespeare and Ben Jonson, and acquainted himself with the circumstances of the recent War of the Theatres, in which Shakespeare had "purged" Jonson. He saw that the public feud had not broken up the friendship of the two men. Applying his theory that a picture should tell as much of a story as possible, he proposed to show on one canvas the

131

two poets as friends playing a game of chess. Chess was extremely popular, and the artist had reason to be confident that all who saw his work would quickly catch the significance in his picturing Shakespeare at the moment of checkmating his friend. Shakespeare no doubt approved of van Mander's intention. While Jonson may have required some persuading before he would let himself be represented as the defeated one, it is likely that he felt pleased at the opportunity of being pictured for posterity with Shakespeare, whose poetry, he was convinced, would be immortal, "not for an age, but for all time."

Planning the picture, van Mander cut, or had a carpenter cut for him, lengths of wood for the stretcher frame, the outside measurements of which were exactly 38 by 30 English inches. After the picture was painted, or after its composition was sketched in, he felt that he had not left enough space above the heads of the two men, and to enlarge the canvas he added a strip of wood $\frac{3}{4}''$ thick outside on the top of a stretcher frame, and thus incorporated into the surface of the picture, part of the canvas that had been folded over the top edge.*

Putting into the picture "divers objects which are allegorically significant of the characteristic qualities of the persons," van Mander placed a book, two inkwells and two quill pens on the table behind the two men to show that the chess players were authors. Visible on the back of the book in Latin script such as a writer would use, but not in letters such as ordinarily would be on the back of a book, is "taff" or "staff," presumably the end of a name. Touching the second "f" is a pen lying precariously across the corner of the book, and looking like a little flagstaff with a flag of surrender. Was this suggestion of a fall a hinting at the first syllable of Falstaff? If so, it was good fun, aiming the name of the comic fat man in Shakespeare's plays at Ben Jonson, who was paunchy, who wrote of his "mountain-belly," and who eventually weighed 278 pounds.

Behind the man on the left in the Chess Picture and slanting down from the upper left corner, are the beginnings of three inscriptions, the endings of which are cut off by the man's figure and

---

* The precise dimensions in English inches are evidence that the wood for the stretcher frame was cut to linear measure in a country where not the Dutch, but the English foot rule was at hand, and that after the composition was sketched in, the enlargement was also made with the English foot rule.

are to be guessed at by the beholder. The top inscription begins with a capital letter which van Mander made puzzling, for it may be either "M" or "N" and it is followed by "o s t" plus two or three indistinct letters. It is possible to read the first inscription as "Nostras" ("our"), which would signify Shakespeare, as it was the adjective applied to him in *The Return from Parnassus II* and by various of his contemporaries; or as "Mostru," meaning monster, which would apply to Ben Jonson who, having often been teased about his unhealthful and monstrous appearance, and being characteristically given to reproaching others with his own defects, used the word "monster" excessively. Monster appears nineteen times in his two *Every Man* plays, and he called Shakespeare's characters "monsters." Shakespeare ridiculed the use of the word monster in Act 3, Scene 2 of *Troilus and Cressida*.

There is some apparent similarity between the second and third inscriptions.* We shall return to the second inscription later.

The man on the left is unquestionably Ben Jonson, as we know from the portraits of him, one of which, the Honthorst portrait, was painted from life some sixteen years or so after the Chess Picture. Allowance must be made for the difference in Jonson's age. The Bodleian Library copy of the Honthorst portrait, especially in the eyes, makes the identification easy.

Ben Jonson was scorbutic, a heavy drinker, a trencherman and wencher. In *Satiromastix* his face (that of Horace in the play) was described as "a most ungodly face . . . like a rotten russet-apple, when it is bruised." He had a "face of pocky holes and pimples," a "parboiled-face." He was a "staring leviathan," a "hollow-cheek'd scrag" with a "brown-bread-mouth"—"such a terrible mouth, that thy beard's afraid to peep out." If "hollow-cheek'd" sounds incompatible with our knowledge that Jonson was corpulent, observe that the Chess portrait shows a creased and pinched-in

---

* The third inscription reads "Parma." Helen Noë,[6] writing without any reference to the Chess Picture, implies that van Mander had some contact with or special interest in Parma, a city celebrated for a school of painting, the Principal of which was called "Il Parmeggianino." Was there some connection here with van Mander, who was himself a principal of a school of painting? Van Mander, in his "Didactic Poem," expressed admiration for Parmeggianino. But it is possible that the third stroke of the fourth letter was a later addition, and that the third inscription as van Mander made it was "Parna," the beginning of "Parnassus," which had direct associations with the two poets and their stage feud.

133

hollow in his cheek, perhaps less accentuated than it appeared in actuality; for we may assume that van Mander, while not striving to flatter, portrayed him at his best. The Honthorst portrait also shows Jonson with corpulent features and sunken cheeks. Discounting the exaggeration of caricature in *Satiromastix*, it remains clear that Jonson had a face aged by hard living. Van Mander slightly modified Jonson's face, particularly through a slight shortening of the nose. The other features, according to the Honthorst portrait, are all correct, even to the cut of the hair.

Thomas Fuller wrote: "Many were the wit-combates between him [Shakespeare] and Ben Jonson, which two I behold like a *Spanish great Gallion* and an *English man of War*; Master Jonson (like the former) was built far higher in learning; Solid but Slow in his performance. Shakespeare, with the English-man of War, lesser in bulk, but lighter in sailing, could turn with all tides, back about and take advantage of all winds, by the quickness of his wit and invention."[7] Showing Jonson being checkmated, van Mander pictures the other man victorious and whistling as he makes the winning move. There has not been an actual game, but the artist in his storytelling device has pictured the man on the left as having taken three pawns, one rook, one bishop, and one knight, while the man on the right, though he has taken only one knight, is the winner, putting his knight on QR3.

The Chess Picture tells us that the man on the right was not only a writer, but an actor. (Ben Jonson ceased to be an actor in 1597.) Van Mander wrote: "Make more art of clothes. . . . Adapt clothing to the dignity of each person, such as will properly represent his profession."[8] The gaudy livery of a King's Player, completely red, with breeches fringed at the bottom, and red hose, marked Shakespeare's profession, but to show him wearing such a garb in a portrait would not befit the dignity of a great poet. The livery, nevertheless, gave van Mander an opportunity to show that the chess player on the right was a King's Player. The artist introduced the complete red livery in the only way he could, and still preserve "the dignity of each person," by picturing close at the actor-author's side a watcher garishly attired from head to foot in red. We are shown a touch of the edge of a hat, and below it, one elbow resting on one knee, with the bottom of the breeches and hose, and the ankle of that leg crossed over his other knee.

134

Among the King's Players only two were authors: Shakespeare and Robert Armin. A contemporary engraving of Armin shows him with features very different from those of the man on the right in the Chess Picture.[9] Thus, by elimination, we identify the man on the right.

He is also with certainty identified in yet another way. The bony structure of his face matches the facial structure of the Darmstadt Death-Mask which has been established as that of William Shakespeare of Stratford.[10] Compare with the Chess Picture the photograph of the death mask in three-quarter position. The two match even to a minor detail of a malformation or pinched area midway along the nasal column on the left side. The comparison leaves no room for doubt that the death mask was that of the man represented in the portrait. With the livery of a King's Player, and an inkwell and a quill pen, the artist who painted the Chess Picture testifies that the actor, William Shakespeare, and the author, William Shakespeare, were one and the same person. Painted one hundred and sixty-five years before the first skepticism was published, the picture is overwhelmingly evidence against the theory that somebody else wrote the plays ascribed to Shakespeare.

The earliest record we have of the Chess Picture is that it was purchased in the 1870s by Colonel Ezra Miller of Mahwah, New Jersey. He told a friend that his investigations had convinced him of the genuineness of the picture, and he prized it above everything he possessed. After his death, when his house burned, the documents which traced the picture's previous history perished, but the painting itself was saved. From Colonel Miller's estate it was acquired in 1900 by the father of the recent owner, the late Mr. Frank de Heyman of Brooklyn, New York. The Chess Picture is now in the possession of Mr. Frank de Heyman's son, the Reverend William de Heyman. Those who handled Colonel Miller's estate had accepted it as a picture of Ben Jonson and Shakespeare.

The elder Mr. Heyman never saw any red color in the picture; it is obvious that Colonel Miller had never seen any; and Mr. Frank de Heyman did not know the red color was there until 1931 when he had the picture professionally restored. He engaged an internationally known specialist, Mr. Stephen S. Pichetto, a restorer of old paintings frequently employed by the Metropolitan Museum of Art, to remove the rotted and decomposed canvas and transfer

135

6

the painting to a new canvas, and to remove the layers of restorers' paint and of varnish that had been applied at several times in past centuries.* Mr. Pichetto's work uncovered the area of red color at the right-hand side of the picture, and it also discovered Karel van Mander's signature near the upper right corner.

Some have argued that a picture of Ben Jonson and Shakespeare painted from life would not have been for years hidden away, but the history of art collecting shows several instances of important paintings lost sight of for decades and subsequently discovered. The Chess Picture has not been hidden away during the past century. It has been given publicity in magazine articles and by a published book, Tracy Kingman's *An Authenticated Contemporary Portrait of Shakespeare* (1932).

The Chess Picture is unquestionably from the early seventeenth century, according to all the experts who have examined it.

A categorical statement by a specialist is accepted as reliable by many, and anyone who contradicts it has to paddle against the current. But where it is a signpost pointing in the wrong direction, it must be challenged. Dr. M. H. Spielmann was, in the early twentieth century, reputed to be the leading authority on Shakespearean portraiture. Referring to early nineteenth-century forgeries by Holder and Zincke, he said in the *Encyclopaedia Britannica*, eleventh edition, 1910: "With these pictures, apparently, should be ranged the composition, now in America, purporting to represent Shakespeare and Ben Jonson playing chess." That Spielmann made this bare assertion without giving any reason for it is shocking enough; but what is more reprehensible is his dismissal of the Chess Picture without his ever having set eyes upon it. A judgment sight unseen in the field of art is indefensible. The greater a man is held to be as an authority, the more scrupulous one supposes he

---

* At all stages of Pichetto's work, Dr. Maximilian Toch, Professor of Industrial Chemistry at Cooper Union and Professor of the Chemistry of Artistic Painting at the National Academy of Design, made photographic studies and x-ray and micro-chemical analysis of the canvas. By chemical tests, Dr. Toch ascertained that the original pigments in the Chess Picture were Black, Burnt Umber, Flake White, and Trieste Vermilion (sulphide of mercury). The fact that there had been several restorations through the centuries showed that the owners of the picture had considered it to be of great importance. The original painting had been applied upon glue sizing, a characteristic of the early seventeenth century previous to Rembrandt.

would be about confirming his judgments of works of art to those he has seen. Spielmann derived his first and published opinion of the Chess Picture from hearsay, since he had not even seen a photograph of it.

Twenty-five years after Spielmann had made himself vulnerable by his article in the *Encyclopaedia*, Dr. Caroline Spurgeon asked him to give at least one reason for his nonacceptance of the Chess Picture's authenticity. Spielmann replied to Dr. Spurgeon on September 10, 1934, in a letter which is now in the Folger Shakespeare Memorial Library. In it he said he had before him the reproduction in color of the picture which Dr. Spurgeon had sent him. (The first color reproduction had just recently been made.) In his letter Spielmann assembled all the accusations he could contrive. He said of the man at the left in the Chess Picture: "I think the figure is 'faked' from a female. It is hard to imagine that such a man as Ben Jonson would wear the dainty linen sleeve and edging we are shown. The outline of the figure also suggests femininity."

Spielmann went on to say: "It is to me absurd to suppose that two men, such as they are pretended to be, would engage on a game of chess and proceed with it while supporting the board with one hand." His letter then told what he found most disturbing. He had naturally assumed that a portrait of Shakespeare would show the English poet in an English costume, but he found the supposed Shakespeare in "a Spanish hat, un-English collar (the like of which I have never seen on an English portrait)."

The hat may have been in the latest London fashion in 1603–1604; for "a hat which came in toward the end of the century [16th] had a brim, like a sombrero."[11] The Challis Portrait of Shakespeare has a large, wide-spreading Spanish collar, extending from shoulder to shoulder. So Spielmann's observation as to the Spanish character of the hat and collar in the Chess Picture ceases to be an objection, as we shall see, and actually becomes corroborating evidence in favor of the picture's authenticity.

Spielmann went all-Spanish in his criticism of the Chess Picture in his letter to Dr. Spurgeon. Of the "Shakespeare" face he wrote in that letter: "The portrait is a life-portrait of Velasquez."*

---

* Dr. Spielmann looked around for a portrait of Velasquez with which to compare the "Shakespeare" face. He could not point to the Velasquez self-portrait in the picture of the Spanish royal family, for that shows great differences which

137

The term "life-portrait" has only one possible meaning—a portrait painted from life—and Velasquez died in 1660. In calling the "Shakespeare" portrait a portrait of Velasquez painted from life, Spielmann was repudiating the charge he had made in the *Encyclopaedia* that the Chess Picture should be "ranged" with nineteenth-century forgeries.

I asked portrait painters for their opinions as to whether the portraits in the Chess Picture were painted from life. Mrs. Elizabeth Pratt, President of the National Association of Women Artists, who had no previous acquaintance with the picture, instantly said of it: "Dutch in manner," and "of the period of James the First," and "of course painted from life." Wilford S. Conrow, an experienced portrait painter, for many years National Secretary of the American Artists' Professional League, and Chairman of their National Committee on Technic, had never seen the Chess Picture before and had no idea who the two men might be. He instantly exclaimed: "This is a very great composition! Yes, certainly painted from life. It is really a silly question, considering the quality of this picture." Then pointing to the man on the right, Mr. Conrow said: "That man is a very important personage, a man of great intellectual force. The other is more meaty." Mr. Conrow gave it as his opinion that the picture had been painted between 1600 and 1620.

Without exception, as far as I know, it is the unhesitating testimony of portrait painters that whether the two men playing chess posed directly for the easel, or for sketches which were then used for the painting, they had been studied by the artist as living subjects.

In his letter to Dr. Spurgeon, Spielmann put his finger on what was to him a disturbing feature of the Chess Picture, Shakespeare's Spanish type of costume. This explains the second of the inscriptions which slant down from the upper left corner. The initial letter of that inscription is a small "d" with an apostrophe. The letters after it are "a r m a d" and there is other evidence pointing to "d'armad" as the correct reading; for "de Armado—

are instantly obvious. He pointed to the supposed Velasquez behind the horses at the right of the "Surrender at Breda." This—which Spielmann was careful to say was probably by a pupil of Velasquez—faces the same way as the "Shakespeare" face, but the Breda portrait has a narrower forehead, a longer nose, and eyebrows of the two eyes not in so even a line as in the "Shakespeare" face.

W. S." in Elizabethan script was cut in on the wooden panel in the back of the frame, presumably by someone who knew that Shakespeare acted the part of Don Adriano de Armado, the Spaniard in *Love's Labour's Lost*, and that he was portrayed in the costume of that part, with un-English collar and extravagant Spanish hat. It was in keeping with van Mander's theory of portraiture for him to picture Shakespeare in clothes that did "properly represent his profession." Costumes on the Elizabethan stage for the main characters in a play were garbs which the audience would recognize as appropriate.

Since the Chess Picture is an indoor scene, we ask why is there a hat on the head of one man and none on the other? Was it not a graceful concealment of baldness? Did it not also remind beholders of the charge in *Satiromastix* that Horace (Ben Jonson) had "more hair than wit"? Van Mander knew the form of a Spanish hat, having seen many in the Netherlands, and he could have painted such a hat to show Shakespeare as Armado, even if the actor had not worn one when he sat for his portrait. In Act 3 of *Love's Labour's Lost*, Moth refers descriptively to the extended brim of Armado's headgear: "your hat penthouse like, o'er the shop of your eyes." Moth also refers to Armado's "thin belly-doublet," which hints at the slenderness of Shakespeare's midriff, if he acted the part.

Impressed by the painting of the hand holding the chess piece, Mr. Conrow had said: "Look at the motion in that hand! Only one or two artists in a century could express motion like this." The effect of motion is produced by the indefiniteness of the hand with its outline in shadow. Some modern artists represent motion by showing an object in successive positions in space. Movement in a hand was a van Mander speciality.*

* A study of more than thirty of van Mander's works reveals the devices he used to create the illusion of motion. He made a fetish of hands and could draw them with marvelous skill. In "Adam and Eve"[12] Adam's hand is raised and open in a gesture of warning against the serpent in a tree, and the fingers show such light and shadows that they almost blend in with the foliage, and thus appear blurred by motion. In "The Music-making Couple"[13] the hand of the woman plucking the strings seems deformed and raggedly drawn as compared with her other hand, and so also the man's hand plucking the strings. Thus when we look at the whole picture and not at the hands particularly, we receive the impression of moving fingers. So also in "The Jovial Peasant Couple,"[14] a deliberately crude drawing of the fingers of the man's uplifted hands vividly communicates the sense of motion. **139**

The Chess Picture has been increasingly in the limelight, and a conviction has been growing that it is authentic. Professor E. R. Lounsbury in a letter from New Haven, December 25, 1904, wrote of the picture: "The face of Shakespeare, here represented, seems to me the most attractive of the portraits imputed." Professor Alfred Chatain, U.S. Government appraiser of imported paintings, on November 29, 1910, said of the Chess Picture that its canvas, pigments, stratum, style, technique, composition, modeling, colors, and tonality confirm its age. Another appraiser, Theodore D. Coe, on April 5, 1912, said the Chess Picture was "painted in England by a Dutchman who had studied the Italian method," with "every evidence of having been done from life. The artist seems possessed with the sole idea of painting accurate portraits of these two men and with the thought that it were well worth while to do so." The editor of the *Boston Post*, February 16, 1916, said the Chess portrait shows "a much more intellectual person than any of the better known Shakespeare pictures."

Dr. Virginia Gildersleeve in 1934 expressed the opinion that Spielmann ought to pay more attention to the Chess Picture. She wanted Spielmann to come to America and look at it. Upon seeing the painting, Dr. Spurgeon wrote to Mr. de Heyman: "As you look at Shakespeare's sensitive and beautiful face, signs of thought, suffering and experience seem to emerge, just as they do when one is looking at a real person—and the combination of sensitiveness, delicacy, strength and power in the face is very remarkable. In Ben Jonson, on the other hand, one sees quickness, impulsiveness, combativeness, wit and brains." The author of *Shakespeare's Imagery*, Dr. Spurgeon, quoted by Dr. Gildersleeve in her memoirs, *Many a Good Crusade* (1954), said of the Shakespeare in the Chess Picture that his "appearance corresponds more closely than any other known representation of Shakespeare with the personality of the poet which has taken shape in my mind during years of detailed studies of his imagery." Dr. Spurgeon said that from "facts or impressions drawn from the images . . . the figure of Shakespeare which emerges is of a compactly well-built man, probably on the slight side, extraordinarily well co-ordinated, lithe and nimble of body, quick and accurate of eye, delighting in swift muscular movement. I suggest that he was probably fair-skinned and of a fresh color, which in youth came and went easily, revealing his

140

feelings and emotions."[15] Professor E. Bradlee Watson of Dartmouth College has given me permission to quote what he wrote me on March 12, 1957: "It is important for the world to be aware that there is so amiable a likeness, which may very well prove to be that of its favorite poet, to replace the stiff and forbidding caricatures that have created a false impression of his live and human self."

Van Mander ascribed great importance to the forehead in a portrait. A further quotation from his "Didactic Poem" is here applicable: "To the forehead, which the ancients believed to be the temple of Genius, I say we must give heed. Some hold the forehead to be the betrayer of the inner mind, the revealer of one's thought, indeed, the book of the heart by which we may read and examine the soul of man; for wrinkles and scars show a hidden urge within an anxious spirit."[16]

Knowing van Mander's theory of poetic composition of a portrait, there is no other portrait painter of the time we could more devoutly wish to have painted the poet Shakespeare. It is fortunate that Jonson of the wrinkled brow and Shakespeare with the forehead of genius were portrayed by so perceptive an artist. These two are the most important portraits of literary men that have come down to us out of the past. The Chess Picture should be exhibited in all the great museums of the world, so that men everywhere may see William Shakespeare of Stratford as Karel van Mander saw him, as actor, dramatist, and poet, whom he portrayed as a man of essentially integrated personality suffused with a glow of inner harmony.

APPENDIX A
Sleuthing in Shakespeare

"The almanac of my true date."

THE COMEDY OF ERRORS, 1.2.41

I<small>N</small> CONTRAST WITH THE UNCERTAINTY AS TO THE order of composition of the first thirteen of Shakespeare's works, most of the last twenty-eight of his plays were reliably dated, or dated closely enough to justify the assumption that looking into them might reveal a pattern in stylistic development, if such existed.

The first hint at a worthwhile direction of research was suggested by the difference in sound between Shakespeare's early and later writing, as for example in a passage in an early play in which all the lines are end pausing, and in one from a later play in which all the lines are without end punctuation. Read aloud to note the contrast between *The Comedy of Errors* (1.2.43–148) and *Antony and Cleopatra* (5.2.152–160).

Was the increasing flexibility of Shakespeare's style to be

143

6*

measured by his increasing propensity toward lines which have no pause at their ends?

There is, as every actor should know, a very slight oratorical pause at the end of every line of verse. Proper delivery enables the ear of a listener to catch the line endings of the pentameter, which are part of the music of Shakespeare's poetry. Even where there is no end punctuation, an actor should make a slight pause at the end of the line, a pause that he would not make if it were a prose sentence.

What seemed to call for counting in Shakespeare's verse was the frequency with which he wrote a line which has no grammatical or rhetorical pause at its end, a line which a modern editor feels should have no end punctuation. It is a line which flows without interruption into the line which follows it. Such a line I call an open line, and its opposite, an end-pausing or end-punctuated line.*

In my counting of open lines—that is, what should properly be open lines—I eliminated my subjective judgment as to the need for punctuation. I did this by using a text in which all of Shakespeare's writings had been punctuated by the same editor, in accordance with his grammatical reasoning and his esthetic feeling. The text used was that of the Cambridge Edition edited by William Aldis Wright. There can be no universally accepted judgment in regard to punctuation. None such was required, since what was being measured was not the working of a machine but the changes in practice of a poet—no absolutes, but comparative percentages.

The counting of percentages of open lines had been attempted by several students of Shakespeare, but their findings had been faulted by an error in procedure. While we may properly count all the lines of verse in a poem and divide into the number of rhymes to obtain the percentage of rhymed lines, we may not use this method to obtain the percentage of an author's proclivity to lines that need no end punctuation. This is because many lines are in positions which preclude their being without end punctuation. The last line of each speech in a play cannot be without end punctua-

---

* A line which does not require end punctuation is by some called a "run-on" line, or what the French call *enjambement*. But since there are those who insist that any line which properly ends with some weaker point than a period is also, or may be, a run-on line, no purpose is served by clinging to a definition which would in no way affect the findings.

tion, and so also the last line of a sonnet, at least in Elizabethan practice. In some plays there are many single-line speeches, which cannot be without end punctuation. A "percentage" based upon all the lines of poetry in a play does not give an indication of the poet's proclivity to open lines at the time he wrote the play. Only lines in positions which would permit them to be open lines can enter into meaningful computations. And so in my counting, each computation of percentage was arrived at by dividing into the number of lines that the editor had left without end punctuation, the number of lines that, by their positions, were what we may call "possible" open lines.

The method of computing percentages of open lines was tried on a sampling of later plays which are reliably dated at five-year intervals:

	Date	Percent of open lines
RICHARD II	1595–96	22.66
HAMLET	1600–01	27.20
MACBETH	1605–06	38.35
THE WINTER'S TALE	1610–11	48.30

It was rewarding and very exciting to see a pattern emerge—a pattern which seemed to offer a clue to sequential order of composition of all Shakespeare's poetry. The percentage of open lines in his last twenty-eight plays rose from 18.39 percent in *Romeo and Juliet* to over 40 percent in his last seven plays, and over 60 percent in some scenes in *Antony and Cleopatra* and *Henry VIII*. (See the table on p. 152–3.)

The statistical base of my studies was broadened when Dr. James G. McManaway, who had always been a helpful adviser, suggested that a text that would be "better" than Wright's to use for a counting of open lines would be the one edited by Peter Alexander. Alexander showed the faulty punctuation in the Quartos and Folios, and the necessity therefore of having Shakespeare punctuated by modern editors. On page 4 of his "Shakespeare's Punctuation," he quoted the first Cambridge editors, Clark and Glover: "In many places we may almost say that a complete want of points would mislead less than the punctuation of the Folios. The consequence is that our punctuation is very little dependent upon the Folios and Quartos but generally follows the practice which has taken possession of the text of Shakespeare, under the arrangement of the best editors."

Prompted by McManaway to the additional grueling labor (no computer could help) of counting lines in Alexander's editing, I also on my own initiative, and for cross-checking, counted the open lines in the editing by George Lyman Kittredge. Alexander's editing yields more open lines than Wright's. Kittredge's yields slightly more than Alexander's. But since both Alexander's and Kittredge's yield percentages that establish the *same sequential order* as do those in the text edited by Wright, only percentages in Wright's editing are cited. The extra labor had not been wasted, since the findings were corroborated by the editings of three distinguished editors.

My sleuthing seemed to be finished. But not so. Having heard me read a paper on open-line percentages,[1] Professor Irving Linn of Yeshiva University suggested that I count also Shakespeare's syllabic intensity—the frequency of the use of polysyllables.

Most words we use in childhood are of one or two syllables. As our vocabularies become more extensive, we normally begin to use a higher percentage of longer words.* This was likely the case with Shakespeare, who had very little formal education. Fortunately for our study, he was not trained in a university and did not have a learned man's vocabulary of long words acquired in college, as *Tamburlaine I* shows Christopher Marlowe had.

I began counting polysyllables, words of four or more syllables, but discovered they are too few in Shakespeare to furnish significant data. I therefore counted words of three or more syllables, considering only syllables as we scan the verse. I excluded from the count the polysyllabic names of Dramatis Personae like Antipholus, Petruchio, Plantagenet, because their presence had been pre-

---

* Shakespeare's large vocabulary did not necessarily include a large proportion of long words. To the contrary, indeed, the words of three or more syllables in a modern dictionary are at least three times higher percentage-wise than are such words in Shakespeare. The rich variety of his vocabulary is for the most part in words of one or two syllables.

146

determined by the story the playwright had chosen to dramatize. My computations are based on the number of words of three or more syllables per thousand lines of verse.

Syllabic intensity in Shakespeare starts very low and rises through the first dozen works until it has more than doubled. The pattern of it breaks after *The Rape of Lucrece*, but up to that point it corroborates the sequential order shown in open-line percentages.

With two corroborating methods of stylistic measurement I was content, until the remembered music—the oratorical sound of lines in Shakespeare's plays—gave insistent hint of a third method. So sensitive a poet as Shakespeare surely had his ear attuned to the rhythm and sweep of his verses orally delivered. He himself used the word "cadency" (*Love's Labour's Lost*, 4.2.126). The rhythmic sequence of words would not be in his lines if he had not felt it and put it there. He must have felt every pause, even where only a comma was needed. And so I counted the frequency of oratorical pauses in his verse, and in so doing found I had my finger on his poetic pulse.

The oratorical pauses are indicated by all kinds of internal punctuation. External punctuation—that is, periods at the ends of stanzas and speeches—is not included in the count, since these pauses were compelled by stanza length or by the dramatic dialogue. To provide a fair comparison with the nondramatic poems, which are in stanzas of six lines or more in length, my counting of oratorical pauses in the plays was taken from speeches of six lines or more in length.

In the table showing my findings, I give the count of oratorical pauses per thousand lines of verse, in stanzas or speeches of six lines or more.

The difference in punctuation between the First Folio and modern editings was brought into discussion by a friend who was inclined to refuse to accept findings based upon modern editings. I sent him four lines from *Henry VI, Part 3*, but without punctuation, and put him on his honor not to identify them until after he himself had punctuated them as he felt they should be. He made two sentences out of them where Shakespeare (First Folio) made only one. Thus prodded into acceptance of modern editing, my friend, after he had identified the four lines, sent me six different punctuatings of them, no two agreeing as to commas, semicolons, and so forth, but five of the six giving the *same number* of internal punctuations. My friend also sent me his findings as to punctuation in a sonnet he selected at random, No. 130. In this sonnet there are 19 points of punctuation in the original publication, and also the same number (19) in three modern editings. All this was grist to my mill, for the significant feature was not the kind of internal punctuation in Shakespeare, but the frequency, because the frequency revealed the feeling for smoothness of flow or for rhythmic pauses in the poet's inner ear.*

The triple findings in Shakespeare's early plays and narrative

	Inferred or anchor date	Percent of open lines	Syllabic Intensity	Pauses per 1,000 lines
PASSIONATE PILGRIM, poems 1 to 14	soon after marriage	6.41	146	1481
VENUS AND ADONIS	as early as 1586	11.76	209	1382
HENRY VI, PART 3	pre-London, perhaps 1587	13.33	206	1391
THE COMEDY OF ERRORS	about 1587–88	14.23	209	1346
HENRY VI, PART 2	after arriving in London	15.35	255	1334
THE TAMING OF THE SHREW	same year as *Titus Andronicus*	16.16	248	1288
TITUS ANDRONICUS	anchor dated 1589	16.36	248	1281
LOVE'S LABOUR'S LOST	about 1590 or 1591 (?)	17.37	(?)	1291
RICHARD III	about 1590 or 1591 (?)	17.40	279	1256
TWO GENTLEMEN OF VERONA	(?)	18.41	310	1169
HENRY VI, PART 1	Dated by "Talbot" ref. 1592	18.35	322	1132
THE RAPE OF LUCRECE	anchor dated 1593–94	19.37	301	1150

* If Shakespeare returned today and compared the punctuation of his verse in Elizabethan times with the interpretative punctuation by modern editors and considered what their aims were, he would very likely say that modern editors have come closer to his intentions than did the editors of the First Folio and the Quartos.

poems are tabulated below. The oratorical pauses decrease, and the open-line percentages and the syllabic intensities increase. The suggested datings are based upon the evidence in the three statistical columns.

We draw several conclusions:

The *Passionate Pilgrim* poems were written before anything else we have from Shakespeare's pen.

Hitherto it has been generally assumed that *Venus and Adonis* and *The Rape of Lucrece* were composed just previous to publication. A. L. Rowse voices this assumption, mentioning that the dedications of the two poems were made "in the years 1593 and 1594 (written therefore in the years 1592 and 1593)."[2] But this is a non sequitur. A date of printing is no proof of the year of a narrative poem's composition any more than it is of a play's.

All the findings support what has been accepted as fact, that *The Rape of Lucrece* was written in 1593–1594 just previous to its publication. With equal certainty they establish that *Venus and Adonis* was composed about seven years earlier—before any of the canonical plays.*

The early dating of *Venus and Adonis* makes the greatest challenge to previous misconceptions. Anyone who wishes to check the accuracy of my statistics may do so with least effort by counting the open lines in the two narrative poems. Take the total number of lines in each poem, subtract the number of stanzas (since the last line of each stanza is not in a position to be a "possible" open line), and divide into the number of lines to which the editing of William Aldis Wright gives no end punctuation. I have of course double-checked all my statistics.

The findings in the two narrative poems in all three columns differ too greatly to permit of any other conclusion than that Shakespeare had held the manuscript of *Venus and Adonis* for about seven years until he found a patron to whom he wished to dedicate its publication. In his dedication to the Earl of Southampton he called the poem "the first heir of my invention," a statement which we

---

* Seymour M. Pitcher makes a convincing argument in *The Case for Shakespeare's Authorship of "The Famous Victories."* He shows that *The Famous Victories* must have been written as early as 1586. Since it is in prose, my statistical measurements cannot be applied to it.

now know was honest and strictly all-inclusive, and not applying, as some have assumed, merely to his nondramatic poetry. It tells us that *Venus and Adonis* with its hearty lustiness and what Robert Graves calls its "playful silliness" was written before anything else which its author considered worth publishing, and which was of sufficient length to be called an "heir."

The Taming of the Shrew and *Titus Andronicus* run neck and neck in the findings, and must have been written within a few months of each other.

The findings establish the order in which the first four comedies and the first four chronicle histories were written.[3]

No syllabic intensity can be ascertained for *Love's Labour's Lost*, and for an interesting reason. Shakespeare ridiculed the pretentious and excessive use of long words in Armado's letter (4.1.60–82), and in the speeches of Holofernes (4.2.1–24). Up to and including the satire on long words in the first three acts and first two scenes of Act 4, the syllabic intensity is 412, much higher than I have found anywhere else in Shakespeare. After the satire and throughout the remainder of the play, the syllabic intensity is only 234. It would appear that having derided verbal ostentation, the dramatist was on guard against the charge that would be made were he himself guilty of the same thing. It seems safe to assume that with conscious self-purge, or for the sake of dramatic contrast, he refrained from continuing to do what he had shown to be absurd. The poet's normal propensity at the time of writing the comedy is indeterminable, except that it was probably nearer to 234 than to 412.

We shall now see how the plays of Shakespeare's contemporaries serve as "controls" to the findings in Shakespeare.

In Christopher Marlowe we have corroborating evidence of the validity of determining order of composition by percentages of open lines. The pattern in Marlowe is one of retrogression from the freedom of open lines, with his "mighty line" becoming more and more end-stopped. Marlowe's propensity to an increase of end-stopping is a direction of development diametrically opposite to Shakespeare's. This is particularly significant since it compels a new point of view in regard to the notion that Shakespeare imitated Marlowe's style.

Here are findings based upon the editing of Marlowe by Ernest Rhys:

Marlowe's works in generally accepted chronological order	Open-line percentage
TAMBURLAINE I	21.88
TAMBURLAINE II	18.49
THE TRUE TRAGEDY OF RICHARD, ETC.	17.77
EDWARD II	15.04
THE JEW OF MALTA	13.63
MASSACRE AT PARIS	14.91
DR. FAUSTUS	13.99
HERO AND LEANDER, Sestiad One	14.58
HERO AND LEANDER, Sestiad Two	11.83

Rhys used the A text of *Dr. Faustus*. Dr. Leo Kirschbaum shows that the A text was a bad quarto of the B version and that the B text is essentially what Marlowe wrote.[4] However, for our purposes, Kirschbaum's editing goes to so great an extreme in refraining from end-of-line punctuation that a count of open lines in his editing cannot be directly compared with that in the plays edited by Rhys. Percentages in Kirschbaum's editing show Marlowe's verse becoming increasingly end-stopped in the two *Tamburlaine* plays, in *Edward II*, and in *The Jew of Malta*.

In the plays of Ben Jonson also, we have a demonstration that open-line percentages are a valid means of indicating order of composition. In the following table, *Sejanus* is far out of line, but Jonson said in the published version of it that it was partly the work of "a second Pen." The collaborator, it has been believed, was either Shakespeare or Chapman. The percentages show it could have been only one of these. By 1603, when *Sejanus* was published, Shakespeare had barely attained to 31 percent of open lines. If he had collaborated with Jonson in writing *Sejanus*, that play would have a percentage of open lines somewhere between Shakespeare's 31 percent and Jonson's proclivity in 1603, which was 26 percent or 27 percent, or much below the play's actual 35.77 percent. But Chapman's average in *Bussy D'Ambois* in 1604 was 39.32 percent. Chapman's percentage combined with Jonson's could account for the percentage in *Sejanus*.

Jonson's plays	Date	Open-line percentages
EVERY MAN IN HIS HUMOUR	1598	22.63
EVERY MAN OUT OF HIS HUMOUR	1599	22.59
CYNTHIA'S REVELS	1600	23.06
THE POETASTER	1601	25.75
SEJANUS	1603	35.77
VOLPONE	1606(?)	29.18
THE ALCHEMIST	1606(?)	27.09
CATILINE	1611	31.08
THE DEVIL IS AN ASS	1616	31.18

Marlowe's syllabic intensity at the beginning of his career, in *Tamburlaine I*, is 289, almost as high as Shakespeare eventually attained.

As for proclivity to open lines, Shakespeare's percentages of open lines during his early career were not so large as those with which Marlowe began. In Shakespeare's early mid-career they were not so large as those of George Chapman. But considering his entire career, Shakespeare's propensity to open lines began at a lower percentage, increased more rapidly, and went to greater height than did that of any of his contemporaries. This will be seen from the table in Chapter 2 and the following:

	Date	Percentage of proclivity to open lines
ROMEO AND JULIET	1594–95	18.39
RICHARD II	1595–96	22.66
MIDSUMMER NIGHT'S DREAM (Act 4)	1595–96	22.62
KING JOHN	1596–97	27.55
MERCHANT OF VENICE	1596–97	28.05

	Date	Percentage of proclivity to open lines
HENRY IV, PART 1	1597	30.48
HENRY IV, PART 2	1597	31.05
MUCH ADO ABOUT NOTHING	1598 or earlier (?)	26.04
HENRY V	1598–99	29.95
JULIUS CAESAR	1599 or earlier (?)	26.03
AS YOU LIKE IT	1599–1600	27.28
HAMLET	1600–01	27.20
TWELFTH NIGHT	1600–01	28.43
MERRY WIVES OF WINDSOR (Act 4)	1601	28.70
TROILUS AND CRESSIDA	1601–02	28.43
OTHELLO	1604 or earlier (?)	26.68
MEASURE FOR MEASURE	1604 (?)	31.21
KING LEAR	1605	31.12
ALL'S WELL THAT ENDS WELL	(?)	35.50
TIMON OF ATHENS	1605 (?)	36.41
MACBETH	1605–06	38.33
PERICLES (Act 3)	about 1606 (?)	41.79
ANTONY AND CLEOPATRA	1606–07	47.74
CORIOLANUS	1607–08	45.48
CYMBELINE	1609–10	46.90
THE WINTER'S TALE	1610–11	48.30
THE TEMPEST	1611–12	44.28
HENRY VIII	1612–13	43.92

We observe that from about 1597 Shakespeare's stylistic development tapered off and he held to a plateau in proclivity to open lines, and after seven years, about 1603 or 1604 there came a 153 new spurt. From the comparative steadiness of the plateau, we may say with certainty that it was an unconscious proclivity. Stylewise there were three periods in Shakespeare's career: the first up to *Midsummer Night's Dream*; then to the writing of *Othello*; and third from *Measure for Measure* to the end.

As the reader has already been told, my statistical studies in *Like to the Lark* have been based upon the text of the Cambridge Edition, edited by William Aldis Wright. There is no consensus that I have been able to discover among Shakespearean scholars that anyone has edited the complete Shakespearean text to perfection. There are differences of opinion where editors have debated what word the poet intended; as for example, "sight" or "side" in *Passionate Pilgrim* poem 2 and Sonnet 144, "grudges" or "drugs" in *Titus*, 1.1.154, and "observance" or "obeisance" in *As You Like It*, 5.2.105. Because "side" and "obeisance" seem to me to make better sense, I have in those instances quoted from the *Oxford Shakespeare*, edited by W. J. Craig. Also, I have used the text edited by Craig in my discussion of *Passionate Pilgrim* poem 14.

APPENDIX B

Dating the Sonnets

"When I do count the clock that tells the time."

EVERYONE WHO HAS ATTEMPTED TO DATE THE
Sonnets has observed that Sonnet 104 gives evidence
that the bulk of the sonnets to the friend were written over a period
of four years:

> Three beauteous springs to yellow autumn turn'd
> In process of the seasons have I seen,
> Three April perfumes in three hot Junes burn'd,
> Since first I saw you fresh, which yet are green.

With this time spread, Robert Gittings[1] specifies three theories
as to the overall period of composition: 1593–98; 1598–1603; and
"the late 1580s." Chambers dates the sonnets to the friend in 1595–
1599. The guess of A. L. Rowse is that Shakespeare wrote the bulk of
them from 1591 to a "terminal date—Spring 1595." Late daters, by   155

which I mean those who think Shakespeare began writing the sonnets to the friend as late as 1593 or thereafter, interpret in the light of modern longevity expectations, not Elizabethan ones, their author's reference to his own advancing age. Because Shakespeare when he composed his sonnets was "old enough to write about youth with an understanding mind,"[2] the late daters insist that when he began them he must have been about thirty years old.*

Chambers gives a good reason for believing that Shakespeare himself arranged the order of his published *Sonnets*.[5] Hilton Landry says: "On the basis of my examination . . . I must conclude that the order of the Quarto is generally and essentially right, and that the burden of proof rests on those who think otherwise."[6] Many have felt that the sonnets are in logical order, though of course not in order of composition.

Before I began applying statistical measurements to the sonnets, it seemed to me likely that there is a deviation from the order of composition in the positioning of Sonnets 1 to 17, which urge the friend to marry. These give the impression that they were

---

* The early dating of the *Sonnets*, 1586–89, championed by John Leslie Hotson, put "slow learner" theorists on the defensive. I mention Hotson's theory not to marshal its support, but because the findings of open-line percentages, syllabic intensities, and oratorical pauses have a significant bearing upon his theory, although they point to a quite different conclusion. Hotson persuasively dates three "topical" sonnets, Nos. 107, 123, and 124 as referring to happenings in the year 1589 or before.[3] Hotson's dating aroused violent controversy. Several different explanations of Sonnet 107 were offered, the most widely accepted being that the "mortal moon" was Queen Elizabeth who suffered "her eclipse" in her climacteric, illness, or death. But would Shakespeare have dared to refer to the Queen as a "tyrant"? None of the anti-Hotson explanations met all the details in Sonnet 107 as did his explanation that it referred to the defeat of the Spanish Armada which moved through the English Channel in the formation of a horned moon. Gittings thought Sonnet 107 might refer to the defeat by Christians in Hungary of the greatly-feared Turks ("mortal moon") in April 1589, and at first glance his interpretation seemed acceptable, if other considerations were ignored. In the light of those other considerations, however, Hotson's explanation remains the only one that is completely acceptable in all the details.

With the other "topical" sonnets also, Hotson's explanation in each case seems to be the only one that takes into account all the details. And after his theory had been disputed, Hotson was able to bring forward further evidence,[4] in showing that not merely the three sonnets, but four others, Nos. 25, 66, 80, and 86 also point to having been written in 1589 or thereabouts. Hotson assumed that all seven "topical" sonnets belonged to the last year of the four-year time spread.

written some years after the bulk of the sequence, and were placed at the beginning to save the poet's relationship with his friend from imputations of homosexuality. The unprepared-for abruptness with which these seventeen introduce the poet's urging lends credence to this impression. Repetitious in theme beyond all such harping on one string anywhere else in Shakespeare, these first seventeen do serve a purpose, and so one feels that they were placed where they are for that purpose.

Each of the 154 sonnets has 14 lines, except No. 99 which has 15, and No. 126, which has only 12.

Here are the statistical findings in the obvious groups of sonnets and in all the sonnets:

	Percent of open lines	*Syllabic Intensity*	*Pauses per 1,000 lines*
SONNETS, to Dark Lady, 127 to 152	14.50	176	1356
SONNETS, 1 to 154	18.30	253	1216
SONNETS, to the friend, 18 to 126	18.30	275	1199
SONNETS, first seventeen and last two	23.48	—	1100

The first two columns indicate that the first seventeen and last two sonnets were written after the pattern of rising syllabic intensity had broken, and so the syllabic intensity in those sonnets is omitted as valueless.

The statistics in all three columns show that most of the sonnets to the Dark Lady were written before those in the friend section. Only three of the Dark Lady sonnets, Nos. 133, 134, and 144 make any reference to the friend, or to a friend. It seems likely that the final two sonnets, which refer to Cupid, were added later to provide a classical conclusion. If Sonnets 153 and 154 are assumed to have been written at about the same time as the Dark Lady sonnets, then Sonnets 127 to 154 would have an open-line percentage of 15.93 and syllabic intensity of 186, but these numbers would not affect the order of composition.

The surprisingly low syllabic intensity in the Dark Lady sonnets may be ascribable to mental processes and vocabulary associated

157

with physical relaxation in sex activity rather than the greater complexity and higher creativity of the poet's reactions in his love for his friend.

With the above findings and those in Appendix A, the dating of the writing of the sonnets becomes a process similar to threading pearls in order of size to make a graduated string. I suggest that you thread them in where you see that they belong in the table on page 148, and then compare your placement of them with the placement in the table in Chapter Two. Note that all three findings in the sonnets to the friend (Nos. 18 to 126) place the four-year period of their composition as 1589–93.*

The findings indicate that Shakespeare tried his hand at sonneteering (some of the *Passionate Pilgrim* sonnets) as early as at the age of about nineteen. He wrote most of the sonnets volume when he was between twenty-four and twenty-nine years of age. He added the first seventeen sonnets when he was about thirty-two, and no doubt did some revising and polishing after that. All together, he was writing sonnets over a period of at least fourteen years.

---

* In Hotson's seven "topical" sonnets, pauses per thousand lines are 1,264; and the open-line percentage is 13.18. Syllabic intensity in the seven sonnets is 367, but in six of them (omitting No. 66) it is 255. These findings are compatible with Hotson's evidence that these seven had been written as early as he believed they were, but contrary to Hotson's assumption, these findings are evidence that the seven sonnets were not among the last to be written, but among the first.

APPENDIX C

Unexpected Dividend

"Why is Time such a niggard of hair? Because it is a blessing that he bestows on beasts: and what he hath scanted men in hair, he hath given them in wit."

THE COMEDY OF ERRORS, 2.2.80–84

O PEN-LINE PERCENTAGES SHED UNEXPECTED LIGHT on an interesting incident in Shakespeare's later career. Having an obstinate notion that he knew better than anyone how plays should be written, Ben Jonson satirized some of his fellow dramatists in *Cynthia's Revels* (1600), and in *The Poetaster* (1601). In a return barrage in the "War of the Theatres," those who felt they had been attacked, ridiculed Jonson in *Satiromastix*, 1601–02. Soon thereafter, a college play, *The Return from Parnassus II* (Christmas 1602 or earlier) was acted by the undergraduates of St. John's College, Cambridge. It contained these revealing lines: "Here's our fellow Shakespeare, puts them all down, I (aye) and Ben Jonson too. O that Ben Jonson is a pestilent fellow; he brought up Horace giving the Poets a pill, but our fellow Shakespeare hath given him a purge."

What was the purge Shakespeare gave Jonson? There have been several guesses. Now, with no uncertainty, open-line percentages tell us what that purge was.*

We have had various theories as to which dramatists were satirized by what characters in *Cynthia's Revels* and *Poetaster*. H. S. Mallery thinks that "in *Satiromastix* Dekker plainly identifies himself with Hedon of the former play, and Crispinus of the latter." This sounds complicated and confusing. The significance of it, however, is clear. The dramatists who were ridiculed were each satirized by differently-named characters in Jonson's two plays. But why did Jonson thus shift the identities? It was because a major element in the fun for an audience of a satirical play was guessing the identities of those being satirized. Jonson had given the audiences of *Cynthia's Revels* the opportunity to guess at the identities. He changed the names of characters in *The Poetaster* so that its audiences would have the same fun. Would the authors of *Satiromastix* deny the same pleasure to its audiences? Assuredly not. They created a play in which the actual poets represented by the characters were to be recognized only by allusion.

In *Satiromastix*, Horace (Jonson) was "untrussed" (figuratively compelled to let down his clothing after taking a purgative). Dekker did not present himself in the guise of one of the characters who were most effective in the untrussing. He did not need to establish himself as one of those who were outstandingly triumphant over Horace, for he was the accredited author of the play. Had

---

* Some have held that the purge was in the satirical comedy, *Troilus and Cressida*. Their argument is that since Jonson was a worshipper of the classics, he was laid low by this comedy in which Shakespeare challenged the enthusiasms of the classicists by debunking the Homeric heroes and showing the Greek warriors as obstreperous, quarrelsome, and feeble-minded, and the great Achilles as cowardly and dishonorable. Other guesses as to the "purge" Shakespeare administered to Jonson are expressed by Marchette Chute: "It is conceivable that the reference is to some role that Shakespeare, as an actor, took in the company's production of *Satiromastix*. Or it may be that the Cambridge boys thought that Shakespeare was the author of *Satiromastix*, since it was produced by his company and Dekker's name had not yet been identified with it in print."[1] While it was not until later that the text of the play was printed, it was known before the opening that Thomas Dekker and John Marston were among the dramatic poets particularly aggrieved by satire directed at them in *Cynthia's Revels*, and that Jonson had speeded his writing of *The Poetaster* to get it on the stage before those he had satirized could retaliate, as they were preparing to do with *Satiromastix*.

Dekker made himself the chief untrusser he would have appeared cheaply egotistical. Jonson in *The Poetaster* had opened himself to widespread ridicule by presenting himself as the great Horace. Dekker had Jonson's bad example of self-laudation to warn him against making a similar mistake.

If we had been members of the audience at the opening of *Satiromastix*, we would have guessed from Tucca's line: "My name's Hamlet, revenge," that Tucca was Dekker, who in presenting the play was ostensibly wielding the cudgels for the poets Jonson had attacked. This identification would have become a certainty when in the Epilogue we heard Tucca assume the authority of the principal author: "The Capten (Tucca) delivers himself and his prating company into your hands. . . . If you set your hands and Seales to this, Horace will write against it, and you may have more sport. . . . My Poetasters will untrusse him agen, and agen, and agen." We would thus have become convinced of the identification even before Tucca in his final words called the audience "my Twopenny tenants." (The usual 1d. charge for admission would be doubled for an opening.) Later, we would have known that our identification was correct, when we paid 6d. for a printed copy of *Satiromastix* and read its Foreword in which Dekker wrote: "A second Cate-mountaine mewes, and calles me Barren, because my brains could bring foorth no other Stigmaticke than Tucca, whome Horace hath put to making, and begot to my hand." This definite acknowledgement of authorship limited to the part of Tucca, tells us by implication that the other Stigmatickes in the play were conceived of by the other offended poets. At least one of the other poets shaped the part and wrote most or all the lines for the character by whom he was to be represented. This seems to have become an open secret by the time the play was printed, as Dekker's Foreword patently asserts. Alfred Harbage admits the possibility that Dekker was not the sole author: "Jonson's charge that Marston had a hand in it may be well founded although the name of Dekker alone appears on the title page."[2]

Since Dekker was Tucca in *Satiromastix*, and no longer either of the characters Jonson had made him in *Cynthia's Revels* and *The Poetaster*, any of the other "Poetasters" in *Satiromastix* might represent any of the other dramatic poets. If we had been in the audience at the first performance of *Satiromastix*, we would have wondered   161 which person on the stage represented Shakespeare. Long before the end of the performance we would have found a clue in the name and a stronger clue in the temperament of one of the characters. The spokesman and leader of those who untruss Horace is Crispinus.* Crispinus has a less revengeful spirit than the others; he handles Horace with gentleness, giving him a chance to save himself from being purged, until Horace by his obstinacy forces Crispinus to proceed against him; he defeats Horace not by railing but by humorous arguments. (Shakespeare and Jonson were known to be firm friends.) Furthermore, Crispinus speaks the best poetry in the play, and he is twice called "master poet."

This identification is now supported by overwhelming evidence.

By 1601, when *Satiromastix* was being written, the playwrights close to Shakespeare must have realized that if his personality, poetic style, and humor were to be convincingly represented by a character in the play, his part had better be written by Shakespeare himself. Though we may not know all the fun the audience had at the first performance of *Satiromastix*, we have an advantage over the Elizabethans who witnessed its opening, since we can analyze the progressively developing styles of verse in other plays by Dekker and Marston and Shakespeare, not only before but after the date of *Satiromastix*. Here our study of open-line percentages yields an unexpected dividend.

Previous to *Satiromastix*, 1601–02, there are only two plays: *Shoemaker's Holiday* and *Old Fortunatus*, which Dekker is believed to have written without collaboration. There are three plays by Marston whose dates of composition make them valid for purposes of comparison. Here are the percentages of open lines in those plays, and in *Satiromastix*, exclusive of the 150 lines of verse in the Crispinus passages:

	Percent
Dekker's *Shoemaker's Holiday* (before 1600)	13.75
Dekker's *Old Fortunatus* (1600)	17.95
Satiromastix, exclusive of 160 Crispinus lines (1601–02)	17.15
Marston's *Antonio and Mellida* (1599–1601)	19.03
Marston's *What You Will* (1599–1601?)	23.16
Marston's *The Malcontent* (1603–04)	23.99

* Crispinus from the Latin *crispo*, "to brandish" and *spina*, "spike," means "brandish spike," a lovely pun on "shake spear."

Contrast with the opposite the percentages of open lines in Shakespeare:

	Percent
Four plays immediately preceding *Satiromastix*, average	27.47
Hamlet, a few months before *Satiromastix*	27.20
Troilus and Cressida (1602), a few months after *Satiromastix*	28.42
Four plays just after *Satiromastix*, average	30.45

Now let us see where the Crispinus passages in *Satiromastix* fit into the above.

Of the 150 lines of verse in the Crispinus-Horace dialogue, there are 133 lines which are not the final lines of speeches and which therefore could be open lines. Of these, 38 are open lines. The percentage of "possible" open lines which are actually open lines is 28.57 percent.

This is more than half as large again as in the rest of the play. The one hundred and sixty lines were written in a year when Shakespeare's developing freedom had attained to precisely that percentage of open lines, as shown in Appendix A. Dekker's and Marston's characteristic percentages of open lines at that time were very much smaller.

The conclusion seems inescapable that neither Dekker nor Marston could have imitated the style of Shakespeare so perspicaciously and so deceptively as to withstand this modern analysis of the percentages of open lines. The percentage of open lines in the Crispinus-Horace passages not only indicates that those passages were not written by Dekker or Marston, but it carries the same weight of conviction of Shakespeare's authorship as if he had affixed his signature to them.

This study of open-line percentages amply demonstrates that we have here one hundred and fifty lines of poetry plus six short prose speeches, written by Shakespeare, which have not hitherto been recognized as his. A reading of all *Satiromastix* will show how different the hundred and fifty lines of verse are from anything else in the play. They are good comedy, building up the seeming impossibility of defending baldness to heighten the success of the defender.

The lines begin with Crispinus speaking to Horace:

163

CRISPINUS Do we not see fools laugh at heav'n, and mock
    The maker's workmanship? Be not you griev'd,
    If that which you mould fair, upright and smooth,
    Be screw'd awry, made crooked, lame, and vile,
    By racking comments, and calumnious tongues;
    So to be hit it rankles not: for innocence
    May with a feather brush off the foulest wrongs;
    But when your dastard wit will strike at men
    In corners, and in riddles fold the vices
    Of your best friends, you must not take to heart,
    If they take off all gilding from their pills,
    And only offer you the bitter core.

HORACE Crispinus, –

CRISPINUS Say, that you have not sworn unto your paper,
    To blot her white cheeks with the dregs and bottom
    Of your friends' private vices; say, you swear
    Your love and your allegiance to bright virtue
    Makes you descend so low, as to put on
    The office of an executioner,
    Only to strike off the swoln head of sin,
    Where'er you find it standing; say, you swear,
    And make damnation parcel of your oath,
    That, when your lashing jests make all men bleed,
    Yet you whip none: court, city, country friends,
    Foes, all must smart alike; yet court, nor city,
    Nor foe, nor friend, dare winch at you: great pity. . . .

    We come, like your physicians, to purge
    Your sick and dangerous mind of her disease.

DEMETRIUS In troth, we do; out of our loves we come,
    And not revenge: but if you strike us still,
    We must defend our reputations;
    Our pens shall, like our swords, be always sheath'd,
    Unless too much provoked, Horace: if then
    They draw blood of you, blame us not, we are men.
    Come, let thy muse bear up a smoother sail;
    'Tis the easiest and the basest art to rail.

HORACE Deliver me your hands: I love you both,
    As dear as my own soul; prove me, and when
    I shall traduce you, make me the scorn of men.

164   BOTH Enough, we are friends.

Crispinus and Demetrius offer to let the quarrel dissolve in friendship, but Horace, uncured, soon says, "Here be epigrams upon Tucca, divulge them among the gallants; as for Crispinus, that Crispine-ass, and Fannius [Demetrius Fannius] his play-dresser . . . These Poet-apes, their mimick tricks shall serve With mirth to feast our muse, whilst their own starve." As though this were not sufficiently provocative, Horace praises hair and condemns baldness in an attack slanted at Crispinus, and forces Crispinus to untruss him:

HORACE For, if of all the body's parts the head
        Be the most royal; if discourse, wit, judgment,
        And all our understanding faculties,
        Sit there in their high court of parliament
        Enacting laws to sway this humorous world,
        This little isle of man; needs must that crown,
        Which stands upon this supreme head, be fair,
        And held invaluable, and that crown's the hair:
        The head, that wants this honour, stands awry,
        Is bare in name and in authority.

SIR VAUGHAN He means bald pates, mistress Minever.

HORACE Hair, 'tis the robe which curious nature weaves
        To hang upon the head; and does adorn
        Our bodies in the first hour we are born:
        God does bestow that garment; when we die,
        That, like a soft and silken canopy,
        Is still spread over us; in spite of death,
        Our hair grows in our graves, and that alone
        Looks fresh, when all our other beauty's gone.
        The excellence of *hair* in this shines clear,
        That the four elements take pride to wear
        The fashion of it; when fire most bright does burn,
        The flames to golden locks do strive to turn;
        When her lascivious arms the water hurls
        Above the shore's waist, her sleek head she curls;
        And rorid [dewy] clouds, being suck'd into the air,
        When down they melt, hangs like fine silver hair.
        You see, the earth, whose head so oft is shorn,
        Frighted to feel her locks so rudely torn,
        Stands with her hair on end, and, thus afraid,
        Turns ev'ry hair to a green naked blade.   165

Besides, when, struck with grief, we long to die,
We spoil that most, which most does beautify;
We rend this *head-tire* off. I thus conclude,
Colours set colours out; our eyes judge right
Of vice or virtue by their opposite:
So, if fair hair to beauty add such grace,
Baldness must needs be ugly, vile, and base.

SIR VAUGHAN True, master Horace, for a bald reason is a reason
that has no hair upon't, a scurvy, scalded reason.

MINEVER By my truly, I never thought, you could ha' pick'd
such strange things out of hair before.

ASINIUS Nay, my ningle can tickle it, when he comes to't.

MINEVER 'Troth, I shall never be enamel'd of a bareheaded man
for this, what shift soever I make.

HORACE Dare defend baldness?

CRISPINUS I shall win
No praise by praising that, which to deprave
All tongues are ready, and which none would have.

BLUNT To prove that best by strong and armed reason,
Whose part reason fears to take, cannot but prove
Your wit's fine temper, and from those win love.

MINEVER I promise you, h'as almost converted me;
I pray, bring forward your bald reasons, master poet.

CRISPINUS Mistress, you give my reasons proper names;
For arguments, like children, should be like
The subject that begets them; I must strive
To crown *bald heads*, therefore must baldly thrive;
But be it as it can: To what before
Went arm'd at table this force bring I more:
If a *bare head*, being like a dead man's skull,
Should bear up no praise else but this, it sets
Our end before our eyes; should I despair
From giving *baldness* higher place than hair?

166   MINEVER Nay, perdie, hair has the higher place.

CRISPINUS   The goodliest, and most glorious strange-built wonder,
            Which that great architect hath made, is heav'n;
            For there he keeps his court, it is his kingdom,
            That's his best master-piece; yet 'tis the roof
            And ceiling of the world: that may be call'd
            The head or crown of earth, and yet that's bald,
            All creatures in it bald; the lovely *sun*,
            Has a face sleek as gold, the full-cheek'd *moon*,
            As bright and smooth as silver: nothing there
            Wears dangling locks, but sometimes blazing stars,
            Whose flaming curls set realms on fire with wars.
            Descend more low, look through man's five-fold sense;
            Of all, the *eye* bears greatest eminence,
            And yet that's bald; the hairs, that like a lace
            Are stitch'd unto the lids, borrow these forms,
            Like penthouses, to save the eyes from storms.

SIR ADAM   Right, well said.

CRISPINUS   A head and face, o'ergrown with shaggy dross,
            O, 'tis an orient pearl hid all in moss;
            But when the head's all naked, and uncrown'd,
            It is the world's *globe*, even, smooth, and round:
            Baldness is nature's *butt*, at which our life
            Shoots her last arrow; what man ever led
            His age out with a staff, but had a head
            Bare and uncover'd? he whose years do rise
            To their full height, yet not bald, is not wise:
            The *head* is wisdom's house, *hair* but the thatch;
            Hair? it's the basest stubble; in scorn of it
            This proverb sprung,–*He has more hair than wit*:
            Mark you not, in derision how we call
            A head grown thick with hair, *bush-natural*?

MINEVER   By your leave, master poet, but that bush-natural is one
            o' the trimmest, and most intanglingst beauty in a woman.

CRISPINUS   Right, but believe this,–pardon me, most fair,–
            You would have much more wit, had you less hair:
            I could but weary you to tell the proofs,
            As they pass by, which fight on *baldness'* side,
            Than were you talk'd to number on a head
            The hairs; I know not how your thoughts are led;
            On this strong tower shall my opinion rest,
            Heads thick of hair are good, but bald the best.

167

[Crispinus is appointed by the king to declare judgment on Horace.]

CRISPINUS Under control of my dread sovereign,
　　　　　We are thy judges; thou, that didst arraign,
　　　　　Art now prepared for condemnation:
　　　　　Should I but bid my muse stand to the bar,
　　　　　Thyself against her wouldst give evidence,
　　　　　For flat rebellion 'gainst the sacred laws
　　　　　Of divine poesy; herein most she miss'd;
　　　　　Thy pride and scorn made her turn satyrist,
　　　　　And not her love to virtue (as thou preachest:)
　　　　　Or should we minister strong pills to thee,
　　　　　What lumps of hard and indigested stuff,
　　　　　Of bitter *Satyrisme*, of *Arrogance*,
　　　　　Of *Self-love*, of *Detraction*, of a black
　　　　　And stinking *Insolence*, should we fetch up?
　　　　　But none of these; we give thee what's more fit,
　　　　　With stinging nettles crown his stinging wit.

TUCCA Well said, my poetical huckster; now he's in thy handling
　　　　rate him, do rate him well.

HORACE O, I beseech your majesty, rather than thus to be nettled,
　　　　I'll ha' my satyr's coat pull'd over mine ears, and be
　　　　turn'd out o' the nine muses' service.

It is unlikely that Ben Jonson was as dismayed by the purge in *Satiromastix* as Horace describes himself as being, though we have no record of Jonson's writing any plays during the next two years, not until *Sejanus*.

The 165 lines of the above-quoted Crispinus passages were no doubt dashed off in haste to speed the readying of the play. Nevertheless, there are among them some quotable lines, notably those which in their derision of long-haired human specimens, have amazing timeliness. While the verses in these passages are decidedly not great poetry, or poetry of universal import, they do have the quality of veritable Shakespeare in their humor, skillful handling of contrasting personalities, fancifulness, figurative language, and natural phrasing. Without any belittlement to the poet, they may well be accepted into the canon of genuine Shakespeare.

168

SOURCES

Chapter 1

1   Frederick J. Pohl, "The Death-Mask," pp. 115–26.
2   Letters of Thomas Gainsborough to David Garrick, given in *The Private Correspondence of David Garrick*, ed. James Boaden (London, 1831–32), vol. 1, pp. 328–32.
3   E. B. Everitt, *The Young Shakespeare*, Preface.
4   Max Meredith Reese, *Shakespeare, His World and His Work*, p. 37.
5   Benjamin Ifor Evans, *The Language of Shakespeare's Plays*, p. 17.
6   *Ibid.*
7   Sir Edmund Kershever Chambers, *Shakespeare Gleanings*, p. 9.
8   John Mackinnon Robertson, *The Genuine in Shakespeare*, p. 24.
9   Albert Feuillerat, *The Composition of Shakespeare's Plays*, p. 34.
10 Alfred Harbage, *William Shakespeare, A Reader's Guide*, pp. 97, 98.

11   *Ibid.*, p. 98.

12   William Shakespeare, *The Complete Works of Shakespeare*, ed. by G. L. Kittredge (Boston and New York: Ginn & Co., 1936), p. 133.

13   Robert Adger Law, *Shakespeare's Earliest Plays*, p. 105.

14   Thomas Whitfield Baldwin, *William Shakespeare Adapts a Hanging*, pp. 1–11.

Chapter 3

1   Charlotte Carmichael Stopes, *Shakespeare's Family*, p. 15.

2   Harold Grier McCurdy, *The Personality of Shakespeare*, p. 46.

3   Pohl, "The Death-Mask," pp. 115–26.

4   John Seely Hart, "The Shakespeare Death Mask," pp. 304–317.

5   *Calendar Domestic Series, State Papers, 1547–1580* (London: Public Record Office, 1856–72), vol. 1, p. 232.

6   C. Read, *Lord Burghley and Queen Elizabeth* (New York: Knopf, 1960), p. 11.

7   John Henry de Groot, *The Shakespeares and "The Old Faith,"* p. 43.

8   *Ibid.*, p. 142.

9   Oliver Baker, *In Shakespeare's Warwickshire and the Unknown Years*, p. 289.

10   Louis C. Elson, *Shakespeare in Music*, pp. 78, 110, 133.

11   Alan Keen and Roger Lubbock, *The Annotator*, p. 41.

12   Alan Keen, " 'In the Quick Forge and Working-house of Thought. . . . ' *Lancashire and Shropshire and the Young Shakespeare*," pp. 256–76.

Chapter 4

1   Chambers, *Sources for a Biography of Shakespeare*, p. 11.

Chapter 5

1   Comtrolment Roll 219 m. 54 Hilary 26 Eliz.

2   Clara Chambrun, *Shakespeare Rediscovered*, pp. 14, 40–51, 102.

3   Ivor Brown, *The Women in Shakespeare's Life*, pp. 25–26.

4   Peter Alexander, *Shakespeare's Life and Art*, p. 21.

5   *Shakespeare Newsletter* (Kent, Ohio: Louis Marder, Sept. 1951), p. 16.
6   Keen and Lubbock, *The Annotator*, p. 70.
7   Annie Doris Wraight, *In Search of Christopher Marlowe*, pp. 218, 219.
8   Thomas Kay, *The Story of the "Grafton" Portrait of William Shakespeare*, 82 pp.
9   Pohl, "The Death-Mask," pp. 115–26.

Chapter 6

1   Seymour M. Pitcher, *The Case for Shakespeare's Authorship of "The Famous Victories*," p. 112.
2   Shakespeare, *Complete Works*, ed. G. L. Kittredge, p. 1492.
3   J. Q. Adams, *A Life of William Shakespeare* (New York: Houghton Mifflin, 1925), p. 334.
4   L. A. Fiedler, "Some Contexts of Shakespeare's Sonnets," p. 79.
5   C. Wright, "Anthony Mundy, 'Edward' Spenser, and E. K.," *Modern Language Assoc. Publications*, vol. 76, Part 1 (March 1961), p. 36.
6   Law, *Shakespeare's Earliest Plays*, p. 103.

Chapter 7

1   Reese, *Op. Cit.*, p. 189.
2   *Ibid.*, p. 205.
3   Dasent, *Acts of the Privy Council*, XV, p. 141.
4   Wolfgang Clemen, *The Development of Shakespeare's Imagery*, p. 28.
5   C. Wilson, *Bernard Shaw; a Reassessment* (New York: Atheneum, 1969), p. 15.
6   Robertson, *Op. Cit.*, p. 17.
7   Alfred Leslie Rowse, *Christopher Marlowe*, p. 132.
8   Charles Norman, *The Muses' Darling, Christopher Marlowe*, p. 62.
9   Norman Rabkin, *Shakespeare and the Common Understanding*, p. 12.
10 *Cymbeline*, V. 4.158.
11 Sonnet 82.
12 Richard David, *The Janus of Poets*, p. 31.

Chapter 8

1   Robertson, *Op. Cit.*, p. 26.
2   Hereward T. Price, *The Authorship of Titus Andronicus*, pp. 55–81.
3   In a letter to the author from Mrs. Geraldine Huston of Teaneck, N.J., July 28, 1967.
4   Muriel Clara Bradbrook, *Shakespeare and Elizabethan Poetry*, p. 110.
5   William Stearns Davis, *Life in Elizabethan Days*, p. 238.
6   Reese, *Op. Cit.*, p. 203.
7   Richard Simpson, ed., *The School of Shakespeare*, p. 356.

Chapter 9

1   *Measure for Measure*, 1.4.60–61.
2   Allison Gaw, *The Origin and Development of 1 Henry VI*, p. 60.

Chapter 10

1   W. G. Ingram and Theodore Redpath, *Shakespeare's Sonnets*, Sonnet 99.
2   In a letter to the author from Dr. Celeste Wright, University of California at Davis, May 7, 1968.
3   Clive Staples Lewis, *English Literature in the Sixteenth Century Excluding Drama*, pp. 504–505.

Chapter 11

1   W. S. Holdsworth, *History of English Law*, 13 vols. (Boston: L. B. 1922–52), p. 504.
2   Henry McClure Young, *The Sonnets of Shakespeare; a psychosexual analysis*, pp. 1–121.
3   McCurdy, *Op. Cit.*, pp. 1–223.
4   George W. Knight, *The Mutual Flame on Shakespeare's Sonnets and The Phoenix and the Turtle*, p. 37.
5   R. Ardrey, *African Genesis* (New York: Atheneum, 1961), p. 346.
6   Lewis, *Op. Cit.*, p. 505.

Chapter 12

1   A. Lynch, "Shakespeare Found Out!", *Book Monthly* (London), vol. 14 (1919), pp. 543–46.

2   M. M. Mahood, *Shakespeare's Wordplay*, p. 89.

3   *Ibid.*, pp. 89, 102, 103.

Chapter 14

1   Ivor Brown, *Dark Ladies including Shakespeare's Dark Lady*, p. 269.

2   Chambers, *William Shakespeare. A Study of Facts and Problems*, p. 562.

3   Hilton Landry, *Interpretations in Shakespeare's Sonnets*, p. 130.

4   W. Frayne, *Mr. Shakespeare of the Globe*, p. 24.

5   Ingram and Redpath, *Op. Cit.*, pp. 3, 4.

6   Reese, *Op. Cit.*, p. 410.

7   Rowse, *Shakespeare's Sonnets*, p. xi.

8   *Ibid.*, p. xvii.

9   John Leslie Hotson, *Mr. W. H.*, p. 136.

10   Lewis, *Op. Cit.*, p. 503.

11   Pohl, "On the Identity of 'Mr. W. H.,' " p. 43.

12   Hotson, *Mr. W. H.*, p. 25.

13   *Ibid.*, p. 158.

14   *Early History of the Houghton Family*, reprinted from an ancient book (London: The Mitre Press, 1931), p. 18.

Chapter 15

1   "Shakespeare's $4\frac{1}{2}$ yards of red cloth on March 15, 1603–4," *New Shakespeare Society Transactions in 1877–79*, Appendix, pp. 11–20.

2   John Nichols, *Progresses, Processions and Magnificent Festivities of King James the First.* Stephen Harrison, *The Arches of Triumph Erected in honour of the High and Mighty Prince James the First . . .*

3   Thomas Dekker, *Dramatic Works*, pp. 267–75.

4   Karel van Mander, Dutch and Flemish Painters, tr. C. van de Wall (New York: McFarlane, Warde, McFarlane, 1936), pp. 88–92.

5   Karel van Mander, *Das Lehrgedicht,* sections V 36, V 30, V 43, V 88.

6   Helen Noë, *Carel van Mander en Italie,* p. 68.

7   Reese, *Op. Cit.,* p. 382, Note 1.

8   Karel van Mander, *Das Lehrgedicht,* section X 3.

9   Engraving of Robert Armin, Picture Collection, New York Public Library.

10   Pohl, "The Death-Mask," pp. 115–26.

11   Lucy Barton, *Historic Costumes for the Stage* (Boston: Walter H. Baker Co., 1935), p. 219.

12   Elizabeth (Valentiner) Paatz, *Karel van Mander als Maler,* Plate XIV.

13   *Ibid.,* Plate XXIX.

14   *Ibid.,* Plate VI.

15   V. C. Gildersleeve, *Many a Good Crusade* (New York: Macmillan, 1954), pp. 240–46.

16   Karel van Mander, *Das Lehrgedicht,* section VI 29.

Appendix A

1   Pohl, "The Shakespeare Quadricentennial: The Poet's Growth," lecture given before the Andiron Club of New York City, April 17, 1964.

2   Rowse, *Shakespeare's Sonnets,* Introduction, p. xxvii.

3   There has been much controversy as to not only the date but the authorship of *Henry VI, Part 1.* A. D. Wraight, in *In Search of Christopher Marlowe,* believes it to have been written in collaboration by Marlowe, Peele, Greene, and Alleyn. But C. F. T. Brooke presents strong evidence that Shakespeare was the original and sole author. In the First Folio all the chronicle histories were printed in order of historical sequence, and the three parts of *Henry VI* were thus numbered 1, 2, and 3. "On November 8, 1623, the publishers of the Shakespeare Folio, Blount and Jaggard, entered our play (*Henry VI, Part 1*) for publication under the rather surprising title of 'The Thirde parte of Henry ye Sixt.' The work now known as *1 Henry VI* is certainly meant, for *2* and *3 Henry VI* (in their early forms) had both been previously licensed, and the Blount-Jaggard license specifically refers

only to such of Shakespeare's plays 'as are not formerly entred to other men.' It is probable that in thus listing as the third part the drama which by historical sequence became in the Folio the first part, the publishers meant more than simply that this was the last part remaining unlicensed. It seems fair to assume that they so thought of it because they remembered it as the latest of Shakespeare's *Henry VI* plays to be presented on the stage." (C. F. T. Brooke, *The Yale Shakespeare: The First Part of King Henry the Sixth*, pp. 136, 137).

4   L. Kirschbaum, *The Plays of Christopher Marlowe* (Cleveland and New York: Meridian Books, 1962), pp. 461–64.

Appendix B

1   R. Gittings, *Shakespeare's Rival* (London: Heinemann, 1960), pp. 1–138.
2   Bradbrook, *Shakespeare and Elizabethan Poetry*, p. 146.
3   Hotson, *Shakespeare's Sonnets Dated*, pp. 107, 123–24.
4   Hotson, "More Light on Shakespeare's Sonnets," pp. 111–18.
5   Chambers, *William Shakespeare. A Study of Facts and Problems*, p. 562.
6   Landry, *Op. Cit.*, p. 130.

Appendix C

1   Marchette Chute, *Ben Jonson of Westminster*, p. 110.
2   Harbage, *Shakespeare and the Rival Traditions*, p. 108.

7*

SELECTED BIBLIOGRAPHY

Acheson, Arthur. *Shakespeare's Lost Years in London 1588–1592.* New York: Brentano's, 1920.

Adams, Joseph Quincey. *A Life of William Shakespeare.* New York: Houghton Mifflin, 1925.

Alden, Raymond MacDonald. *English Verse.* New York: H. Holt, 1903.

Alexander, Peter. "Shakespeare's Pronunciation." *Brit. Acad., London. Annual Shakespeare Lecture, 1945.*

———. *Shakespeare's Life and Art.* London: J. Nisbet & Co., 1939.

Armstrong, Edward Allworthy. *Shakespeare's Imagination.* Lincoln: University of Nebraska Press, 1963.

Austin, Warren E. "A Supposed Contemporary Allusion to Shakespeare as a Plagiarist." *Shakespeare Quarterly*, Vol. 6, no. 3 (Autumn, 1955), pp. 373–80.

Bakeless, John. *Christopher Marlowe.* New York: William Morrow, 1937.

Baker, Howard. *Induction to Tragedy. A Study in a Development of Form in Gorboduc, The Spanish Tragedy and Titus Andronicus.* University, La: Louisiana State University Press, 1939.

Baker, Oliver. *In Shakespeare's Warwickshire and the Unknown Years.* London: Simpkin Marshall, 1937.

Baldwin, Thomas Whitfield. *On the Literary Genetics of Shakespeare's Plays 1592–1594.* Urbana: University of Illinois Press, 1959.

———. *The Organization and Personnel of the Shakespeare Company.* Princeton: Princeton University Press, 1927.

———. *William Shakespeare's Petty School.* Urbana: University of Illinois Press, 1943.

———. *William Shakespeare Adapts a Hanging.* Princeton: Princeton University Press, 1931.

Bathurst, Charles. *Remarks on the differences in Shakespeare's versification in different periods of his life* . . . London: J. W. Parker & Son, 1857.

Besant, Sir Walter. *London in the Time of the Tudors.* London: A. & C. Black, 1904.

Bolton, Joseph S. G. "Titus Andronicus: Shakespeare at Thirty." *North Carolina University, Studies in Philology,* Vol. 30 (1935), pp. 208–24.

Boughner, Daniel C. "Don Armado and the Commedia dell' arte." *North Carolina University Studies in Philology,* Vol. 37 (1940), pp. 201–24.

Bowden, Henry George. *The Religion of Shakespeare.* London: Burns and Oates, 1899.

Bradbrook, Muriel Clara. *The School of Night. A Study in the Literary Relationships of Sir Walter Ralegh.* Cambridge: Cambridge University Press, 1936.

———. *Shakespeare and Elizabethan Poetry. A Study of his Earlier Work in Relation to the Poetry of His Time.* London: Chatto and Windus, 1951.

Brooke, Charles Frederick Tucker, ed. *The Shakespeare Apocrypha.* Oxford: Clarendon Press, 1918.

————. *The First Part of King Henry the Sixth.* New Haven: Yale University Press, 1918.

Brown, Ivor. *Dark Ladies including Shakespeare's Dark Lady.* London: Collins Clear-Type Press, 1957.

————. *The Women in Shakespeare's Life.* New York: Hill and Wang, 1969.

Butler, James Davis. "The Vocabulary of Shakespeare." *Wisconsin Acad. of Sciences, Arts and Letters. Transactions.* Vol. 14, Pt. 1. (1903), pp. 40–55.

Byrne, M. St. Clare. *Elizabethan Life in Town and Country.* London: Methuen, 1925.

Campbell, Oscar James. *Shakespeare's Satire.* London, N.Y., etc.: Oxford University Press, 1943.

Chambers, Sir Edmund Kershever. *Shakespeare Gleanings.* London: Oxford University Press, 1944.

————. *Sources for a Biography of Shakespeare.* Oxford: Clarendon Press, 1946.

————. *William Shakespeare. A Study of Facts and Problems.* Oxford: Clarendon Press, 1930.

Chambrun, Clara (Longworth) Comtesse de. *Essential Documents never yet presented in the Shakespeare Case.* Bordeaux: Delmas, 1934.

————. *Shakespeare Rediscovered. By means of Public Records, Secret Reports and Private Correspondence Newly Set Forth as Evidence on His Life and Work.* New York & London: Charles Scribner's Sons, 1938.

Chute, Marchette G. *Ben Jonson of Westminster.* New York: Dutton, 1953.

Clemen, Wolfgang. *The Development of Shakespeare's Imagery.* Cambridge: Harvard University Press, 1951.

Cordley, Clifford. "Shakespeare and Sport." *Bailey's Magazine of Sports and Pastimes* (London). Vol. 119 (Jan.–June, 1923), pp. 178–82.

David, Richard. *The Janus of Poets. Being an essay on the dramatic Value of Shakespeare's Poetry both good and bad.* Cambridge: Cambridge University Press, 1935.

179

Davis, William Stearns. *Life in Elizabethan Days*. New York: Harper & Bros., 1930.

Dawson, Giles Edwin. *The Life of William Shakespeare*. The Folger Shakespeare Library, Washington, D.C., 1958.

De Groot, John Henry. *The Shakespeares and "The Old Faith."* London: King's Crown Press, 1948.

Dekker, Thomas. *Satiromastix. Dramatic Works*, Vol. 2. Cambridge: Cambridge University Press, 1953–55.

Drinkwater, John. *Shakespeare*. London: Duckworth, 1953.

Elson, Louis C. *Shakespeare in Music*. Boston: L. C. Page, 1900.

Evans, Benjamin Ifor. *The Language of Shakespeare's Plays*. London: Methuen, 1966.

Everitt, E. B. *The Young Shakespeare. Studies in Documentary Evidence.* Copenhagen: Rosenkilde and Bagger, 1954.

Feuillerat, Albert. *The Composition of Shakespeare's Plays*. New Haven: Yale University Press, 1953.

Fiedler, Leslie A. "Some Contexts of Shakespeare's Sonnets." *The Riddle of Shakespeare's Sonnets*. New York: Basic Books, 1962.

Fleay, Frederick Gard. *A Chronicle History of the Life and Work of William Shakespeare, player, poet, and playmaker*. London: J. C. Nimms, 1886.

Ford, Malcolm. "Shakespeare and Jonson. A recently discovered portrait of the two Elizabethan poets by Karl van Mander." *Arts and Decoration*, Vol. 4 (1914), pp. 450–51.

Fort, James Alfred. *The Two Dated Sonnets of Shakespeare*. London: Oxford University Press, 1924.

Fripp, Edgar Innes. *Shakespeare, Man and Artist*. London, New York: Oxford University Press, 1938.

Gascoigne, George. *Certayne Notes of Instruction in English Verse*. London, 1575. Reprint. London: A. Murray & Son, 1868.

Gaw, Allison. *The Origin and Development of 1 Henry VI*, University of Southern California Language and Lit. Series. First Series, No. 1. Los Angeles: University of Southern California, 1926.

Greg, Walter Wilson. *The Editorial Problem in Shakespeare. A Study of the Foundation of the Text*. Oxford: Clarendon Press, 1951.

Halliday, P. B. *A Shakespeare Companion 1550–1950*. New York: Funk & Wagnalls, 1952.

Haney, John Louis. *The Name of William Shakespeare*. Philadelphia: Egerton Press, 1906.

Harbage, Alfred. *Conceptions of Shakespeare*. Cambridge: Harvard University Press, 1966.

———. "Dating Shakespeare's Sonnets." *Shakespeare Quarterly*, Vol. 1, No. 2 (April 1950), pp. 57–63.

———. *Shakespeare's Audience*. New York: Columbia University Press, 1941.

———. *Shakespeare and the Rival Traditions*. New York: Macmillan, 1952.

———. *William Shakespeare: A Reader's Guide*. New York: Farrar, Straus, 1963.

Harrison, George Bagshawe. *Introducing Shakespeare*. New York: Penguin Books, 1939, 1957, 1966.

———. *Shakespeare at Work*. London: G. Routledge & Sons, 1933.

———. *Shakespeare Under Elizabeth*. New York: Holt, 1933.

Harrison, Stephen. *The Arches of Triumph Erected in honour of the High and mighty prince James, the First of that name at His Majesties entrance and passage through . . . London upon the 15th day of March 1603*. London: Stephen Harrison, printed by I. Windet, 1604.

Hart, John Seely. "The Shakespeare Death Mask." *Scribner's Monthly*, Vol. 8 (July, 1874), pp. 304–17.

Hastings, William T. "The New Critics of Shakespeare. An Analysis of the Technical Analysis of Shakespeare," *Shakespeare Quarterly*, Vol 1 (July 1950), pp. 165–76.

Heywood, Thomas. "The Earls of Derby and the Verse Writers and Poets of the 16th and 17th Centuries." *Chatham Soc. Remains, History and Literature of Lancaster and Chester*, Vol. 29 (1953), pp. 11–20.

Hotson, John Leslie. *The Death of Christopher Marlowe*. Cambridge: Harvard University Press, 1925.

———. *Mr. W. H.* New York: Knopf, 1964.

———. *Shakespeare's Sonnets Dated, and other essays*. London: Oxford University Press, 1949.

Hotson, John Leslie. "More Light on Shakespeare's Sonnets," *Shakespeare Quarterly*, Vol. 2, No. 2 (April 1951), pp. 111–18.

Houghton, Alexander. Will in *Chatham Soc. Publ.*, Vol. 51 (1860), pp. 237–41.

Houghton, John Wesley. *Houghton Genealogy.* New York: F. H. Hitchcock, 1912.

Huys, E. "Carl van Mander peintre, poete et historigraphe," *Koninklijke Geschied-en ondheidkundige Kring van Kortrijk. Hanlingen.* Nieuwe reeks, deel 15, Courtrai, 1936, pp. 117–92.

Ingram, W. G. and Redpath, Theodore. *Shakespeare's Sonnets.* London: University of London Press, 1964.

Isaacs, J. "Shakespeare's Earliest Years in the Theatre." *Brit. Acad., London. Annual Shakespeare Lecture, 1953.*

Jarratt, John Ernest. "The Grafton Portrait." *John Rylands Library Bulletin.* (Manchester, Eng.) Vol. 29 (1945), pp. 225–28.

Kalff, Gerrit. *Geschiedenis der Nederlandsche Letterkunde.* Vol. 3, Groningen: J. B. Walters, 1907. pp. 387–410. (Biographical account of Karel van Mander).

Kay, Thomas. *The Story of the "Grafton" portrait of William Shakespeare "aetatis suae 24, 1588" with an account of the sack and destruction of the Manor House of Grafton Regis by the Parliamentary forces on Christmas Eve 1643.* London: S. W. Partridge & Co., 1914.

Keen, Alan. " 'In the Quick Forge and Working-house of Thought. . . .' Lancashire and Shropshire and the Young Shakespeare." *John Rylands Library Bulletin.* Vol. 33, No. 2 (March 1951), pp. 256–70.

Keen, Alan and Lubbock, Roger. *The Annotator. The Pursuit of an Elizabethan Reader of Halle's Chronicle Involving some Surmises About the Early Life of William Shakespeare.* London: Putnam's, 1954.

Kingman, Tracy. *An Authenticated Contemporary Portrait of Shakespeare.* Mount Vernon, N.Y.: William E. Rudge, 1932.

Knight, George Wilson. *The Mutual Flame on Shakespeare's Sonnets and The Phoenix and the Turtle.* London: Methuen, 1955.

Landry, Hilton. *Interpretations in Shakespeare's Sonnets*. Berkeley: University of California Press, 1963.

Law, Robert Adger. *Shakespeare's Earliest Plays*. Royster Memorial Studies. Chapel Hill: University of North Carolina Press, 1931.

Lewis, Clive Staples. *English Literature in the Sixteenth Century Excluding Drama*. Oxford: Clarendon Press, 1954.

Mahood, M. M. *Shakespeare's Wordplay*. London: Methuen, 1957.

McCurdy, Harold Grier. *The Personality of Shakespeare. A Venture in Psychological Method*. New Haven: Yale University Press, 1953.

Morgan, Appleton. "Our Debt to Mrs. Shakespeare." *Catholic World*, Vol. 117 (1923), pp. 163–73.

———. "The 'Passionate Pilgrim' Affair." *Conservative Review*, Vol. 3 (1900), pp. 270–77.

Muir, Kenneth, *Shakespeare's Sources*. London: Methuen, 1957.

Nesbit, Ulric. *The Onlie Begetter*. London: 1936.

Ness, Frederic W. *The Use of Rhyme in Shakespeare's Plays*. New Haven: Yale University Press, 1941.

Nichols, John. *Progresses, Processions and Magnificent Festivities of King James the First*, Vol. 1. London: J. B. Nichols, 1828.

Noë, Helen. *Carel van Mander en Italie*. 'S-Gravenhage: Martinus Nijhoff, 1954.

Norman, Charles. *The Muses' Darling, Christopher Marlowe*. New York, Toronto: Rinehart & Co., 1946.

Norris, J. Parker. "The Death Mask." *American Bibliopolist* (New York). February 1875.

———. *Portraits of Shakespeare*. Philadelphia: Robert M. Lindsay, 1885.

Ogden, William Sharp. *Shakespeare's Portraiture*. London: Quaritch, 1912.

Paatz, Elizabeth (Valentiner). *Karel van Mander als Maler*. Strassburg: J. H. E. Heitz, 1930. (Complete reproduction of Karel van Mander's paintings and drawings).

183

Parrott, Thomas Marc. "Further Observations on Titus Andronicus." *Shakespeare Quarterly*, Vol. 1, No. 1 (January 1950), pp. 22–29.

Partridge, Eric. *Shakespeare's Bawdy. A Literary and Psychological Essay and a Comprehensive Glossary.* London: Routledge, 1947.

Pitcher, Seymour M. *The Case for Shakespeare's Authorship of "The Famous Victories."* Binghamton State University of New York, 1961.

Pohl, Frederick J. "The Death-Mask." *Shakespeare Quarterly*, Vol. 12, No. 2 (Spring 1961), pp. 115–26.

———. "On the Identity of 'Mr. W. H.'" *Shakespeare Newsletter* (Kent, Ohio), Vol. 8, No. 6 (December 1958), p. 43.

Pollard, Alfred William. "Shakespeare's Hand in the Play of Sir Thomas More." *Shakespeare Problems*, Vol. 2. Cambridge: Cambridge University Press, 1923.

Price, Hereward T. "The Authorship of Titus Andronicus." *Jour. of English and Germanic Philology* (Urbana: University of Illinois). Vol. 42 (1943), pp. 55–81.

———. "Shakespeare as a Critic." *Philology Quarterly* (Iowa City), Vol. 20 (1941), pp. 390–99.

Proctor, W. G. "The Manor of Rufford and the Ancient Family of the Heskeths." *Hist. Soc. of Lancashire and Cheshire. Transactions. 1907.* Vol. 59 (n. s. 23).

Puttenham, Richard (or his brother George). *The Arte of English Poesie.* London: printed for Richard Field, 1589.

Rabkin, Norman. *Shakespeare and the Common Understanding.* New York: The Free Press, 1967.

Rand, Conyers. *Lord Burghley and Queen Elizabeth.* New York: Knopf, 1960.

Reese, Max Meredith. *Shakespeare his world and his work.* London: Edward Arnold, 1953.

Rendall, G. H. *Personal Clues in Shakespeare Poems and Sonnets.* London: J. Lane, 1934

Robertson, John Mackinnon. *The Genuine in Shakespeare: a conspectus.* London: G. Routledge & Sons, 1930.

Roesen, Bobbymann. "Love's Labour's Lost." *Shakespeare Quarterly,* Vol. 14, No. 4 (October 1953), pp. 411–26.

Rowse, Alfred Leslie. *Christopher Marlowe. His Life and Work.* New York: Harper, 1964.

———. *Shakespeare's Sonnets.* New York: Harper, 1964.

Ryan, Richard. *Dramatic Table Talk, or Scenes, Situations & Adventures Serious and Comic in Theatrical History and Biography,* Vol. 2. London: John Knight and Henry Lacey, 1825.

Scott-Giles, Wilfred Charles. *Shakespeare's Heraldry.* London: J. M. Dent & Sons, 1950.

"Shakespeare's 4½ yards of red cloth on March 15, 1603–04." *New Shakespeare Society Transactions in 1877–79,* Pt. 3, Publ., Ser. 1, Appendix, pp. 11–20. London, 1880.

Sherborn, Charles Davies. *A History of the Family of Sherborn.* London: Mitchell & Hughes, 1901.

Simpson, Richard, ed. *The School of Shakespeare . . . with an account of Robert Greene, his prose works, and his quarrels with Shakespeare.* London: Chatto and Windus, 1878.

Sisson, C. J. "The Mythical Sorrows of Shakespeare." *Brit. Acad., London. Annual Shakespeare Lecture, 1934.*

Smart, John Semple. *Shakespeare Truth and Tradition.* New York: Longmans, Green & Co., 1928.

Spencer, Haselton. *The Art and Life of William Shakespeare.* New York: Harcourt, Brace & Co., 1940.

Spencer, Theodore. *Shakespeare and the Nature of Man.* New York: Macmillan, 1942.

Spurgeon, Caroline F. E. *Shakespeare's Imagery and What It Tells Us.* Cambridge: Cambridge University Press, 1939.

Stokes, Henry Paine. *An Attempt to Determine the Chronological Order of Shakespeare's Plays* (The Harness Essay 1877), London: Macmillan, 1878.

Stopes, Charlotte Carmichael. *Shakespeare's Family. Being a Record of the Ancestors and Descendants of William Shakespeare.* London: Elliot Stock, 1901.

———. *Shakespeare's Warwickshire Contemporaries.* Stratford-on-Avon: Shakespeare Head Press, 1907.

Stopes, Charlotte Carmichael. "The True Story of the Stratford Bust." *Monthly Review* (London). Vol. 15, No. 43 (April 1904), p. 150.

Sweet, George Elliott. *Shakespeare: The Mystery*. Stanford California: Stanford University Press, 1956.

Talbert, Ernest William. *Elizabethan Drama and Shakespeare's Early Plays*. Chapel Hill: University of North Carolina Press, 1963.

Taylor, Rupert. *The Date of Love's Labour's Lost*. New York: Columbia University Press, 1932.

Thurston, Herbert. "The Mr. W. H. of Shakespeare's Sonnets." *Month* (London). Vol. 156 (1930), pp. 425–37.

Toch, Maximilian. A manuscript report on Karel van Mander's Chess Portrait, prepared for Frank de Heyman, in possession of the de Heyman Family.

Van Mander, Karel. *Das Lehrgedicht* [Didactic Poem], German tr. R. Hoecker. Haag: M. Nijhoff, 1916.

Ward, B. R. *The Mystery of "Mr. W. H."* London: C. Palmer, 1923.

Watson, Foster. *The Old Grammar Schools*. New York: Putnam's, 1916.

Webbe, William. *A Discourse of English Poetrie Together with the Author's judgment touching the reformation of our English Verse*. London: printed by John Charlewood for Robert Walley, 1586.

Willcock, Gladys D. "Language and Poetry in Shakespeare's Early Plays." *British Acad., London. Annual Shakespeare Lecture, 1954*.

Willoughby, Edwin Eliott. *A Printer of Shakespeare: the books and times of William Jaggard*. London: P. Allan & Co., 1934.

Wilson, Frank Percy. "Shakespeare and Diction of Common Life." *Brit. Acad., London. Annual Shakespeare Lecture, 1941*.

Wilson, Thomas. *Arte of Rhetorique*. Printed by John Kingston, 1560. (New edition; it was first published in 1553.)

Wislicenus, Paul. *Dokumente zu Shakespeares Totenmaske*. Jena: E. Diederichs, 1911. 44 pp.

———. "The Finest Picture of Shakespeare." Ms. 97 pp. +2 Appendix. (The manuscript is in the possession of the de Heyman family.)

———. *Nachweise zu Shakespeares Totenmaske. Die Echtheit der Maske.* Jena: E. Diederichs, 1913.

Wivell, Abraham. *An Inquiry into the History, authenticity, and characteristics of the Shakespeare portraits* ... London: the author, 1827.

Wraight, Annie Doris. *In Search of Christopher Marlowe. A Pictorial Biography.* New York: Vanguard Press, 1965.

Young, G. M. "Shakespeare and the Termers." *Brit. Acad., London. Annual Shakespeare Lecture, 1947.*

Young, Henry McClure. *The Sonnets of Shakespeare; a psycho-sexual analysis.* Menosha, Wisconsin: George Banta Publishing Co., 1937.

187

INDEX